BRITAIN & EUROPE

BIRDS

by

CHARACTER

The Fieldguide to Jizz Identification

Illustrated by
Ian Wallace, Darren Rees
John Busby, Peter Partington

Written by Rob Hume

PAPERMAC

First published 1990 by
PAPERMAC
4 Little Essex Street London WC2R 3LF
and Basingstoke
Associated companies in Auckland, Delhi, Dublin,
Gaborone, Hamburg, Harare, Hong Kong,
Johannesburg, Kuala Lumpur, Lagos, Manzini,
Melbourne, Mexico City, Nairobi, New York,
Singapore and Tokyo

Conceived, edited, designed and produced by
Duncan Petersen Publishing Ltd,
5 Botts Mews, London, W2 5AG

A CIP catalogue record for this book is available
from the British Library

ISBN 0333490541

Typeset by SX Composing Ltd, Rayleigh, Essex
Printed in Spain by Graficas Estella S.P.A

Who painted what

Ian Wallace: waders, and most of the smaller passerines, including the wagtails, pipits, buntings, warblers and tits.

Darren Rees: large predators, shrikes, chats and miscellaneous passerines.

John Busby: sea birds and smaller predators.

Peter Partington: ducks, geese and game birds.

Contents

Enjoying this book

We created **Birds by Character** for all types of birdwatcher, at all levels of experience, from the beginner to the most competitive lister. The overriding purpose was to convey more fully than ever before the general *character* – or jizz – of most British and European birds. Jizz is instantly appreciated, but its meaning is understood only through experience. This book aims to be the ultimate tool for gaining exactly that experience.

It will reassure you that birds can be enjoyed without learning an alarming number of facts. Start by testing yourself, and the book, on a bird like the blackbird or song thrush. Forget, for a moment, its field marks and colours, and look afresh at the bird's size, shape, behaviour and essential character. See the bird in terms of its jizz – identify it by its character. Then look at other, similar species on nearby pages in the same way and see how they differ.

You will find that you will quickly sharpen your powers of observation and your appreciation of the birds. You will notice more, and what you see will be more memorable. The brain finds it particularly easy to hold a visual impression when it is combined with a verbal perception – each one is a 'peg' for the other. You may well discover that you can 'record' astonishingly fleeting impressions of birds, and that these impressions 'stick' in a reassuring way, building up into the multiple images of a species that add up to its jizz. We believe that the early use of jizz will be especially helpful to young birdwatchers, indeed to anyone nervous of cluttering the mind. Enjoy your birdwatching, use, develop and be proud of your identification skills, test yourself if you like, and you will become more appreciative of each bird's character. You will train both your eye and your mind's eye to make rapid, yet certain, identifications.

If you are already keenly interested in birds, you can still improve your skills and make a fresh start in your efforts to look at birds in terms of jizz. Relax your mind's eye until it receives general character freely and easily. Use the drawings, which illustrate more information about bird behaviour and character than any conventional field guide. The book will widen your horizons and increase your enjoyment of birds, which are so essentially full of life and action. If you like seeing rarities, and have a creditable British list, you may still not yet have looked at the birds themselves in such a way that you see the whole being, rather than a collection of field marks, wing bars, primary projections, tail patterns and so on. **Birds by Character** is our contribution to redressing the balance of bird identification and restoring interest in the bird as a whole, as a living, exciting, absorbing creature.

The authors
March 1990

Basic birdwatching

This is the briefest summary we can contrive of practical points to assist you in actually going out to identify birds. But there is no substitute for an individual approach, to suit your favoured terrain, built up by trial and error.

■ Consult the local weather forecast. Strong winds make small birds keep to cover and are worse than rain.

■ For a visit to the shore, check tide times; waders concentrate at roosts around high tide.

■ In any season, start early. The first two hours of daylight are best for birds; avoid the afternoon lull.

■ Stop and watch; sit down and keep still. Birds lose their shyness of human presence after a few minutes and re-emerge from cover. But in woods and farmland outside the breeding season, search around for flocks.

■ Move slowly, pausing often. Approach bends in tracks, ends of hedges, ditch or stream crossings, woodland edges, with care; look around corners.

■ Use your ears as well as your eyes. Sounds give birds away, even if you can't identify the call.

■ Try to use whatever cover there is, or at least stand against it, in open areas.

■ Make notes. Write them up as fair copies at home.

■ Read books, watch wildlife films, study photographs – do your home-work.

■ If possible, go out with an expert.

Using this book

Species included All the species that breed in Britain; all winter visitors; all passage migrants, plus the most regular rarities — usually those recorded in Britain 30 or more times. Also included is a selection of species restricted to mainland Europe.

Order of species generally follows the taxonomic list used in ordinary field guides, but where appropriate, birds of similar appearance have been grouped together for ease of comparison.

To find a bird you cannot put a name to, flick through the pages looking for groups of birds of similar size, shape and colour to the one you have seen, then explore the plates in depth and compare what you have noted in the field with what is drawn and described.

To look up a species you already know, consult the index on pages 166-174.

The main illustration area contains the images of jizz. They range from pencil sketches, through more detailed drawings to partly, or lightly, coloured images. Rather than show every feather detail or field mark, they are intended to convey the maximum possible amount of character, form and movement. The drawings are complemented by the captions and vice versa.

The smaller, coloured images are secondary to the main illustrations and give basic plumage patterns and field marks. They are useful 'footnotes', but no more: a key to the colours that contribute to bird identification. For fuller plumage details, you must see a conventional field guide or handbook. We suggest, for each species, the best ones to consult – see **cross references**.

Distribution maps show the status of each species in the following categories:

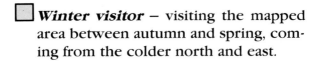

■ *Resident* – staying in the mapped area all year.

□ *Summer visitor* – coming to the mapped area in the spring, breeding, and leaving for the south again in the autumn.

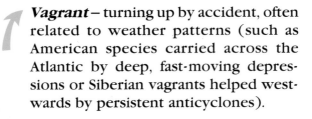

■ *Winter visitor* – visiting the mapped area between autumn and spring, coming from the colder north and east.

Vagrant – turning up by accident, often related to weather patterns (such as American species carried across the Atlantic by deep, fast-moving depressions or Siberian vagrants helped westwards by persistent anticyclones).

Some birds are passage migrants, pausing on the way north in spring and south in autumn, but neither nesting nor staying during the winter months. The range of such species is shown by the same colour code as for winter visitors and the words spring/autumn included.

The information on these maps, together with the **habitat** notes below them, should be studied before any final identification is made. If the bird you suspect is in the wrong place, at the wrong time, or in the wrong habitat, check it again.

Calls (rather than song) are included where possible and where useful, with an attempt at a phonetic impression of the sound made by the bird. There is no written substitute for a sound recording – or the real thing.

The captions describe the main features of the jizz of each species, giving:
a general size comparison with others on the same page;
a general observation; bill, head, wing and tail shapes;
behaviour or characteristic actions;
flight actions and social behaviour.

ABBREVIATIONS	
♂	male
♀	female
juv(s)	juvenile(s)
imm(s)	immature(s)
ad(s)	adult(s)

Scale is generally maintained within the larger images of each plate or within family series of plates, but not throughout the book. To check size, consult a conventional guide.

Cross references to other books are given for every species. These are, in the opinion of the author, the best popularly available references. Jizz is an essential, under-rated aspect of bird identification and in many situations is all you need to know. But it is not the *whole* story, especially in some difficult families with birds of similar character and form. Plumage marks and even complete plumage details are needed to complete the identification process. For these, and for further information, we have given abbreviated cross references as follows:

HTV = *The Macmillan Field Guide to Bird Identification*, by Harris, Tucker and Vinicombe (Macmillan)

PHM = *A Field Guide to the Birds of Britain and Europe*, by Peterson, Mountfort and Hollom (Collins)

LWS = *The Shell Guide to the Birds of Britain and Ireland*, by Ferguson-Lees, Willis and Sharrock (Michael Joseph)

FBI = *Frontiers of Bird Identification*, by Edited by Sharrock (Macmillan)

BB = *British Birds* monthly magazine

PJG = *Gulls, a Guide to Identification*, by P J Grant (Poyser)

Standard reference for all birds of prey — *Flight Identification of Raptors*, by Christenson, Nielson, Porter and Willis (T & A D Poyser).

Latin names follow the taxonomy of Voous, 1973-7.

Parts of a bird mentioned in the captions concentrate not on feather tracts, but on physical shape and form. These are shown on the diagram below.

Knowledge of the correct names of individual feathers and feather tracts is, however, essential and can of course be gained from reputable conventional field guides.

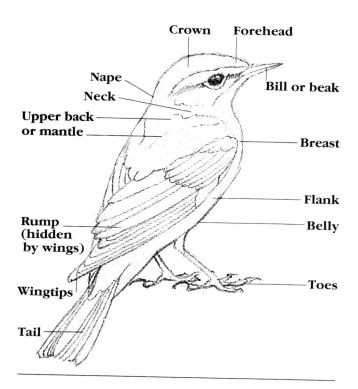

Crown   Forehead

Nape

Neck

Bill or beak

Upper back
or mantle

Breast

Flank

Rump
(hidden
by wings)

Belly

Wingtips

Toes

Tail

Loud, quacking *kwuk kwuk kwuk* in flight
HTV 9; BB 79:365

juv

winter

Red-throated diver
Gavia stellata
Long and low, rather slight, snaky. ● Slender bill from
sloping forehead; bulbous head and bill point upwards.
● Dives from surface with neat forward roll; sits up on water
to flap wings, rolls over to preen. ● Flight low; looks
stretched, hump-backed; wing-beats deep, quick, stiff.

Breeds on remote pools; feeds and winters
on sea.

winter

winter

summer

summer

summer

Black-throated diver
Gavia arctica

Wailing calls in summer
HTV 9; BB 79:365

Large, long, elegant, narrow-bodied. ● Bill dagger-like, held
level with snaky, smoothly-rounded head; recalls guillemot.
● Thick neck held erect; head club-shaped from behind.
● Flight low, straight, wing-beats quite deep; quick, but no
manoeuvrability.

Breeds on large lakes; winters in coastal
bays.

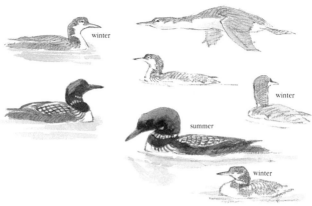

Great northern diver

HTV 10; BB 79:365

Gavia immer

Big, long-bodied, very broad-beamed; always impressive.
● Bill long, heavy, angled, level with big, angular head;
steep forehead sometimes with bump. ● Dives with long
forward roll, wings flicked open as it goes under. ● Flight
fast, straight; hump-backed, wings narrow, central, angled,
beats shallow; legs trailed.

Sandy bays; estuaries, inshore waters.

White-billed diver

HTV 10; BB 79:365

Gavia adamsii

Big and heavy; impressive. ● Bill deep-based, straight
above, angled below, on large head with bump on forehead;
bill and head tilt upwards on thick neck. ● Flight strong,
straight, thundering along on shallow wing-beats; large feet
trailed behind.

Coasts, rare vagrant from Arctic.

Little grebe

Tachybaptus ruficollis

Winnying trill

winter flock

Tiny, fluffy bundle with no tail, floats like a cork. ● Short bill, abrupt forehead to small round head. ● Thin, often erect neck. ● Dives often, suddenly disappears. ● Flight fast but weak, usually short and low, pattering over water.

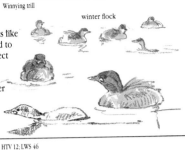

Black-necked grebe

HTV 12; LWS 46

Podiceps nigricollis

Small, rotund, no tail. ● Bill thin, fractionally upcurved; triangular, peaked head. ● Surprised, anxious look in winter. ● Head hunched down or up on thin neck. ● Wispy 'ears' of breeding plumage droop down. ● Fast, low flight lacks agility.

winter

Slavonian grebe

HTV 12; LWS 46

Podiceps auritus

Small, round, no tail. ● Bill straight, evenly tapered. ● Smooth head profile; neck long when erect, but often hunched. ● Flared 'ears' of breeding plumage fan out backwards. ● Open face in winter.

winter   spring

Little Grebe	**Black-necked grebe**	**Slavonian grebe**

Reedy pools, rivers; winters on larger lakes.   Luxuriant weedy lakes; winters in estuaries.   Remote lakes with sedge-beds; coastal in winter.

Slavonian grebe

winter

summer

summer

Red-necked grebe

HTV 15; LWS 44

Podiceps grisegena

Large, long-bodied, solid grebe. ● Thick, heavy, dagger-like bill; large, round head firmly on top of thick, straight neck. ● Suspicious, furtive expression.

Reed-fringed lakes; coastal in winter.

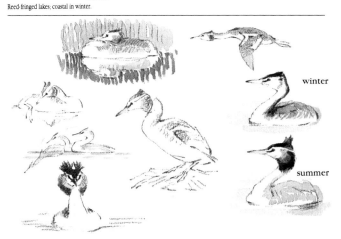

winter

summer

Great crested grebe

Croaks and growls
PMH 38; LWS 45

Podiceps cristatus

Big, elegant, slim grebe. ● Slender, pointed bill on triangular or peaked head set forwards on long, thin, snaky neck. ● Unique 'head-dress' in summer. ● Dives cleanly with slight roll. ● Flight direct, low; looks long, slim wings whirring, outstretched neck and trailing feet drooped. ● Large flocks in winter.

Large lakes, broad rivers; also sea coast.

21

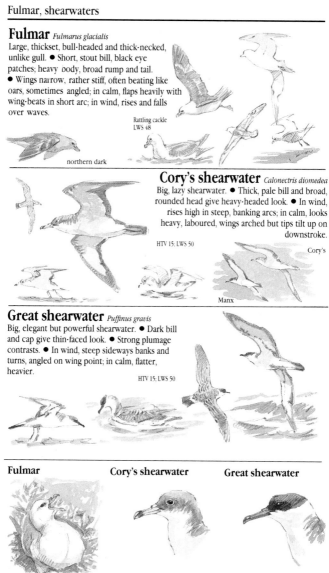

Fulmar *Fulmarus glacialis*

Large, thickset, bull-headed and thick-necked,
unlike gull. ● Short, stout bill, black eye
patches; heavy body, broad rump and tail.
● Wings narrow, rather stiff, often beating like
oars, sometimes angled; in calm, flaps heavily with
wing-beats in short arc; in wind, rises and falls
over waves.

Rattling cackle
LWS 48

northern dark

Cory's shearwater *Calonectris diomedea*

Big, lazy shearwater. ● Thick, pale bill and broad,
rounded head give heavy-headed look. ● In wind,
rises high in steep, banking arcs; in calm, looks
heavy, laboured, wings arched but tips tilt up on
downstroke.

HTV 15; LWS 50

Cory's

Manx

Great shearwater *Puffinus gravis*

Big, elegant but powerful shearwater. ● Dark bill
and cap give thin-faced look. ● Strong plumage
contrasts. ● In wind, steep sideways banks and
turns, angled on wing point; in calm, flatter,
heavier.

HTV 15; LWS 50

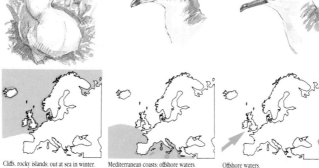

Fulmar   **Cory's shearwater**   **Great shearwater**

Cliffs, rocky islands; out at sea in winter.   Mediterranean coasts; offshore waters.   Offshore waters.

22

Sooty shearwater

LWS 50; HTV 18

Puffinus griseus

Large, dark, seemingly 'mechanical'
shearwater. ● Slim bill and head but heavy,
bulbous body. ● Narrow, long, angled wings
beat stiffly between glides; long, sweeping
turns.

Manx shearwater *Puffinus puffinus*

Quite large, highly contrasted, thin-faced. ● Flight
quick, active; silhouette cross-shaped. In wind, rises
and falls in steep, banking glides; in calm, flat against
surface, sea, short glides between bursts of stiff wing-
beats. Often flies in long, narrow lines.

HTV 17; BB 78:123

Little shearwater

Puffinus assimilis

Small, auk-like, open-faced. ● Flight
rather direct and low, fast, stiff wing-
beats in regular bursts; short glides.
● Patters and flutters over waves.
● Wings slightly rounded or paddle-
shaped.   BB 78:123

Sooty shearwater   Manx shearwater   Little shearwater

Offshore waters.   Breeds on islands; otherwise often off   Open sea.
                          headlands, at sea.

23

Wilson's petrel

Oceanites oceanicus
Tiny, black with white rump.
● Wings broad, straight, tips
rounded. ● Flight strong,
fluttering, with long, rolling
glides. ● Patters on sea and hops
two-footed with raised or
flat, broadly spread wings
like butterfly; frequent
flickering, darting actions.

Storm petrel *Hydrobates pelagicus*

Tiny, insect-like. ● Slightly rounded
wings, short body, broad round tail.
● Series of swallow-like swoops and
weak flutters over sea. Frequent steep
banks and swirling turns, like wind-
blown leaf; patters on surface with
raised wings.

Leach's petrel *Oceanodroma leucorhoa*

Small. ● Long wings often angled and
deeply bowed. ● Long body tapers to
notched tail. ● Flight buoyant,
bounding, darting; frequent glides and
steep banks like shearwater, also tighter
twists; patters with feet only
occasionally.

Wilson's petrel	Storm petrel	Leach's petrel

HTV 20; BB 76:161	HTV 19; BB 76:161	HTV 19; BB 76:161

Breeds on remote islands; otherwise open sea.	Breeds on rocky islands; otherwise far offshore over sea.	Breeds on remote islands; otherwise at sea.

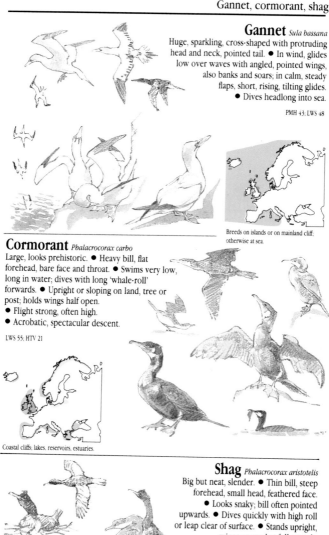

Gannet *Sula bassana*

Huge, sparkling, cross-shaped with protruding head and neck, pointed tail. ● In wind, glides low over waves with angled, pointed wings, also banks and soars; in calm, steady flaps, short, rising, tilting glides. ● Dives headlong into sea.

PMH 43; LWS 48

Breeds on islands or on mainland cliff; otherwise at sea.

Cormorant *Phalacrocorax carbo*

Large, looks prehistoric. ● Heavy bill, flat forehead, bare face and throat. ● Swims very low, long in water; dives with long 'whale-roll' forwards. ● Upright or sloping on land, tree or post; holds wings half open.
● Flight strong, often high.
● Acrobatic, spectacular descent.

LWS 55; HTV 21

Coastal cliffs; lakes, reservoirs, estuaries.

Shag *Phalacrocorax aristotelis*

Big but neat, slender. ● Thin bill, steep forehead, small head, feathered face. ● Looks snaky; bill often pointed upwards. ● Dives quickly with high roll or leap clear of surface. ● Stands upright, wings opened at full stretch. ● Flight very low, quick, direct, few glides.

LWS 54; HTV 21

Breeds on cliffs; otherwise rocky sea shores, headlands.

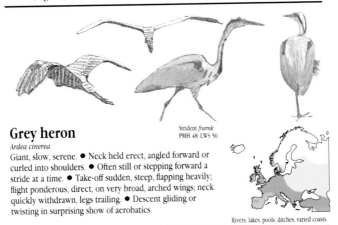

Grey heron

Strident *frannk*
PMH 48; LWS 56

Ardea cinerea

Giant, slow, serene. ● Neck held erect, angled forward or curled into shoulders. ● Often still or stepping forward a stride at a time. ● Take-off sudden, steep, flapping heavily; flight ponderous, direct, on very broad, arched wings; neck quickly withdrawn, legs trailing. ● Descent gliding or twisting in surprising show of aerobatics.

Rivers, lakes, pools, ditches; varied coasts.

Purple heron

HTV 23

Ardea purpurea

Big, elegant, snaky-necked. ● Long, slender bill. ● In flight neck withdrawn in deep pouch; bunched feet obvious; wings narrow-based, with S-shaped trailing edge. ● Flight lighter than grey; dives out of sight into reeds.

Deep reed-beds beside lakes and swamps.

Crane

Trumpeting in flight
PMH 91; LWS 270

Grus grus

Giant, aloof, aristocratic. ● Thin head and bill, often uptilted; long neck thickens into broad shoulders. ● Heavy body, bushy 'tail'. ● Flies with hump-back, neck outstretched. ● Wings long, square, straight and flat; slow beats with rhythmic, slow flick.

Remote marshland, lakes.

imm

ad summer

Wet swampland, flooded grass, reed edges.

Squacco heron

PMH 47. LWS 254

Ardeola ralloides

Rather small. ● Pointed, fairly thick bill, long sloping forehead and long head, merging into thick, loosely feathered neck. ● Oval body with short tail and short, rounded wings; rather short legs. ● Stands motionless in marsh or on floating vegetation, or creeps forward in hunched, sloping posture; stabs head forward after prey. ● Often inconspicuous until taking flight with sudden flurry, going away low into cover.

breeding

Cattle egret

BB 77:451

Bubulcus ibis

Fairly large, upstanding, oval body held clear of medium-length legs. ● Bill short, rather thick, with curved ridge; forehead low but abrupt; chin and throat make obvious jowl. ● Neck medium-length, often hunched and thick; oval, angled body. ● Active feeding, with free walk, short runs with flicking wings; rests in trees, sometimes motionless for hours. ● Flight steady, with head withdrawn, legs trailed, wings broadly rounded and arched.

Pastures, ploughed land, swamps, lakes, thickets.

Little egret

BB 77:451

Egretta garzetta

Slim, dainty, lively. ● Long, dagger bill, long face, snaky neck. ● Head plumes and wispy feathers on back in spring. ● Wades, plunges head-first, dashes after fish with sharp turns, excited, fluttering leaps. ● Flight direct, steady; neck withdrawn, legs trailed.

Muddy creeks; lakes, lagoons, rocky shores.

ads

juv

Night heron

Nycticorax nycticorax

Heavy, dumpy, oval heron. ● Thick bill and squat head and neck shape, hunched into shoulders. ● Shortish legs. ● Thick-necked in flight; wings broadly rounded with soft, padding beats.

Gruff croak
PMH 46

Waterside thickets, pools, fishponds.

♀   ♂

Little bittern

PMH 46

Ixobrychus minutus

Surprisingly small heron type. ● Neat, elegant but slow-moving. ● Dagger bill, thick neck, oval shape; grasps stems and climbs through vegetation. ● Flight quick, with head up, feet down, fast flutter of round wings. ● Leaps up with sudden flurry, crashes back into cover.

Waterside thickets and reed-beds.

landing

Bittern

Deep, resonant boom
PMH 45; LWS 56

Botaurus stellaris

Mysterious and secretive, more heard than seen. ● Strides chameleon-like, body shaking, rocking to and fro. ● Thick neck often erect, head curved over. ● Flight ponderous on broad wings; little neck bump but big, untidy feet.
● Sudden flop down into reeds.

Reed-beds; other swampy places only in winter.

American bittern

LWS 254

Botaurus lentiginosus

Slightly smaller, narrower-winged than bittern. ● Shares upright stance, erect alarm posture. ● Flight freer, more agile; more often in open.

Vagrant from North America

29

White stork

PMH 49; LWS 256

Ciconia ciconia

Huge and impressive. ● Bold stance, body sloping, head up.
● Long, tapering bill on round head, small eye. ● Strides
like a human. ● Flight splendid and magnificent, wings
long, broad, flat. ● Effortless glides, circles very high.
● Low flight heavier, with deep, tiring beats.

Wet farmland, lake edges, lagoons.

Glossy ibis

PMH 49

Plegadis falcinellus

Peculiar, prehistoric. ● Bill thick, evenly down-curved;
head and neck thin. ● Looks heavy-bodied at rest but in
flight strangely skinny, long, with bill/head outstretched,
neck drooped, legs trailed. ● Quick, jerky beats of long,
rounded wings.

Reedy pools, lakes, swamps and floods.

ad

juv

Spoonbill

PMH 50; LWS 57

Platalea leucorodia

Very big, tall. ● Heavy, angled body; short tail depressed.
● Unique bill looks thin, slightly down-curved from side,
spatulate from front, on round head (crested in summer).
● Thick, long legs. ● Bill sweeps water for food, half-open,
in broad arcs. ● Flight direct, quick, a little swan-like; neck
outstretched and slightly drooped; legs trailed.

Reed edge, muddy lagoons, shallow pools.

Mute swan *Cygnus olor*

Very large, long-necked. ● Bill points down from long, solid head on slightly curved or strongly S-shaped neck. ● Tail pointed, often cocked. ● Wings frequently arched. ● Waddling walk on huge, webbed feet, but usually swimming. ● Powerful, direct flight, 'foot-slapping' take-off and landing with 'water-ski' stop.

ad ♂

Whooper swan

Cygnus cygnus

Very, large, long- and often straight-necked; head long and flat but looks small; bill horizontal. ● Open, hard expression. ● Tail short, square, level; wings tightly closed. ● Easy walk, often on grass or ploughed land.

stained

Bewick's swan

Cygnus columbianus

Very large; relatively short- and straight-necked; chunky, goosy form. ● Bill horizontal, on rounder head; concave forehead profile; gentle face. ● Short, square, level tail. ● Easy walk, often on land.

imm

Mute swan

ad

imm

Strangled snort
PMH 51

Whooper Swan

ad

imm

Trumpeting 'whoops'
HTV 25

Bewick's swan

stained

ad

Soft 'hoop hoop'
HTV 25

Fresh water of all kinds, sheltered coasts.

Upland lakes; river valleys, damp pastures.

Extensive floods, lakes, agricultural/grassland.

Pink-footed goose
Anser brachyrhynchus

Large, neat, compact goose. ● Short bill, round head; short, slim neck set high on broad, round body. ● Agile on ground, take-off quick and easy. ● Flight strong, direct; wings long and pointed; in long lines and Vs. ● Twisting, corkscrew descents.

ad

Bean goose
Anser fabalis

Large, handsome, tall and elegant goose. ● Bill long but slim/concave, on rather long head and long neck. ● Long-bodied, heavy but easy walk. ● Flight powerful; in Vs and chevrons.

ad

Greylag goose
Anser anser

Large, heavy, lumbering goose. ● Bill long and heavy, on large, round or angular head, thick neck. ● Deep body; waddling walk and deliberate actions. ● Rises with effort in long, sloping ascent. ● Flight heavy, with big head, broad wings; in irregular masses, Vs and lines.

ad

Pink-footed goose	Bean goose	Greylag goose

Deep *ang ang.* high *wink wink* PMF 52: HTV 27	Deep *abng abng abng* HTV 27	Cackling *abnk abnk abnk* HTV 27

Agricultural and pasture land; lakes, estuaries.	Damp meadows, ploughed fields, stubbles.	Lakes, farmland, reedy swamps, islands.

White-fronted goose

Anser albifrons

Large but agile goose. ● Bill triangular
on square head; short neck; deep chest
giving angular profile. ● Easy, active
walk; instant vertical jump into air and
into fast, fluent flight. ● Flies in long,
wavering lines and Vs. ● Frequent
twisting, whiffling descents.

Yodelling *lyo-lyok*
PMH 53; HTV 27

ad

imm

Estuaries, wet grassland, lakes

Lesser white-fronted goose

Anser erythropus

Small, pretty, neat goose. ● Tiny bill
below steep forehead; round head; long
wings extend beyond tail on ground.
● Easy, light walk; rapid feeding action.
● Flight quick, light.

High yipping cackle
HTV 30

imm

ad

Breeds in thickets, winters on pastures

33

Snow goose

Anser caerulescens

Large, heavy goose. ● Thick, gaping bill, heavy head and long, straight neck give inelegant form. ● Stands tall; easy but twisting walk. ● Flight powerful, direct.

Canada goose

Branta canadensis

Large, long-necked goose. ● Long bill and head. ● Swan-like actions and shape on water. ● Heavy, slightly rolling walk. ● Squabbles. ● Flight heavy but strong, direct, in lines, Vs and irregular packs.

Canada goose, small races

Small, neat, slim-necked. ● Small bill on round or rather long head. ● Easy, agile actions. ● Flight quick and light.

Snow goose	Canada goose, small races	Canada goose

PMH 54

Deep honk
LWS 64

Marshes, wet grassland, stubble fields

Vagrant from North America

Lakes of all kinds; broad rivers, parks.

Brent goose
Branta bernicla

Small, dark. ● Slim bill, rather
long head on chunky neck.
● Forward-leaning on land; on
water, where buoyant, tail-up.
● Feeds in tight groups, upends
in water. ● Size exaggerated in
flight because of heaviness,
broad wings; flies in lines and
amorphous groups, but big
flocks turn in unison.

Rolling *krronk*
PMH 55, LWS 64

dark-bellied

ad

imm

Mudflats, estuaries, salt marshes, coastal
fields.

Barnacle goose
Branta leucopsis

Handsome, striking goose.
● Small, stubby bill on round
head; thick neck. ● Long legs
and quick feeding actions give
easy movements on land.
● Feeds in tight bunches,
sometimes huge flocks
carpeting fields. ● Flight swift,
in irregular packs, wavy lines.

Fast barks
LWS 64

imm

ad

Extensive damp meadows, estuaries.

Egyptian goose

Alpochen aegyptiacus

Tall, rangy, long-legged, unusual goose. ● Slim bill set low on round head, on curved, thin neck high on sloping, large body. ● Quick feeding action, light walk. ● Rather slow, stilted, heavy flight on broad wings.

PMH 55; LWS 66

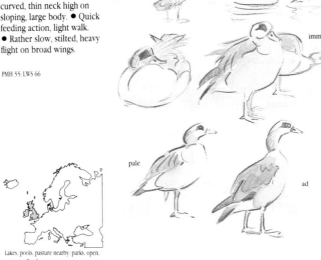

imm

pale

ad

Lakes, pools, pasture nearby; parks, open, wet woodland.

Shelduck

Tadorna tadorna

Large, bulky, rounded, confident. ● Broad, short bill on large, rounded head and short, curved neck. ● Rangy, head-up, half-erect, long-legged, in waddling strides. ● Buoyant on water, often upends, ● Flight steady, heavy, goose-like.

Deep, laughing *ak-ak-ak*
PMH 56; LWS 67

♂

♀

imm

winter ♂

Muddy estuaries; salt marsh; gravel pits.

36

Wigeon

Anas penelope

Medium-sized, round duck with short bill, steep forehead, round head, very short legs, pointed tail.
● Swims high in water, tail-up. ● Flocks graze slowly, heads down. ● Noisy, active; bursts into sudden ascent, or moves to water with angled body, tail down, head thrust forward. ● Flight fast, high; wings pointed, swept back and flickered in shallow action. ● Sudden twisting descent.

Whistled *wheeoo*; growl
PMH 57; HTV 31

Lakes, estuaries, salt and fresh marshes.

winter ♂

♀

American wigeon

Anas americana

Fractionally larger, broader-beamed, squarer-headed than wigeon. ● Neat, short bill on steep forehead; short legs.

HTV 31

♀

winter ♂

Lochs, pools, rivers in moorland; marshes.

Gadwall

Anas strepera

Large, rather long but more compact than mallard. ● Small bill 'stuck' on face; steep forehead; high, curved nape on round head. ● Bill points downwards. ● Sits high in water; flight fast, agile, with rapid beats; glides down to alight.

Nasal *nek-nek*; quack
PMH 57, LWS 70

Quiet rivers, lakes, reservoirs, pits.

winter ♂

♀

Mallard

Anas platyrhynchos

Large, heavy. ● Large, long bill continues forehead profile of big head; tail level or held upwards on water. ● Stands horizontal; waddling, heavy-bellied walk and shuffle. ● Flight fast, direct; wings long, beats below body level. ● Quick descent; glides before settling.

Loud, familiar *quack*
PMH 58

♂ summer

winter ♂

♀

Fresh and saltwater, marshes, parks, stubbles.

Teal

Anas crecca

Small, neat, wader-like. • Small bill
on rather large head with high,
almost flared nape. • Stands
horizontally, deep-bodied, on short
legs. • Easy, waddling walk; quick
nibbling/dabbling feeding action.
• Swims high in water.
• Sudden vertical take-off; flight fast,
twisting; sudden diving change of
height and co-ordinated aerobatics.

Ringing *krik-krik*
PMH 58; LWS 72

♂
summer

♂ winter

♀

Reedy swamps, muddy lake edges, salt
marsh.

Garganey

Anas querquedula

Slightly heavier, more angular than
teal. • Longer, more horizontal bill
and longer head shape. • Easy walk
but low-slung; shy. • Flight slower,
more floating than teal.

Dry rattle
PMH 59; LWS 74; HTV 38

autumn ♂

spring ♂

♀

Freshwater floods, shallow reedy lakes.

Pintail

Anas acuta

Tall, long-necked, elegant in all attitudes. ● Slim, long bill hangs from neat, round head; raised neck pencil-thin. ● Long, pointed tail. ● In flight long and slim; blob-head on thin neck; tapering at both ends. ● Direct, fast, high flight.

PMH 59; HTV 37

♀

winter

Muddy estuaries, salt marsh, stubbles.

Shoveler

Anas clypeata

Rather small but looks heavy, out of proportion, due to shovel-bill, big head. ● Squat, ponderous on water, head hunched, shoulders almost awash. Long, pointed wing tips cross over short tail when upending. ● Deep wing-noise on take-off; flight fast; dangerous look owing to long, heavy head/neck, squat rear.

PMH 60; HTV 41

eclipse ♂

♀

winter ♂

Rich, shallow lakes; reservoirs, salt marsh.

Pochard

Aythya ferina
Medium-sized, neat, well
set-up. ● Long, concave
bill leads smoothly into
high, rounded head. ● Tail
held low. ● Dumpy, rotund on
land. ● Laborious take-off run
from water, then quick but
with no agility; wing-beats
too fast. ● Gregarious.

HTV 47

eclipse ♂

winter ♂

winter ♂

♀

Reedy lakes; reservoirs, gravel pits.

Red-crested pochard

Netta rufina
Big, high-headed and high-
backed; long body. ● Long
slim bill, flared crown;
males splendid, females
dowdy. ● Dabbles and
upends, dives infrequently.
● Flight heavy, wings broad;
recalls dabbling duck.

PMH 61

eclipse ♂

♀

winter ♂

Reedy lakes; shallow lagoons.

Ferruginous duck

Aythya nyroca

Medium-sized, neat, tidy; low in water. ● Slender bill sweeps into long forehead before high peak well back on head. ● Tail up or level. ● Quick, rolling flight.

PMH 62; HTV 48

summer ♂

♀

winter ♂

Reedy lakes, broad rivers.

Ring-necked duck

Aythya collaris

Rather large, heavy. ● Slim bill; peaked forehead, bump on nape. ● Female has questioning, spectacled expression. ● Dives well. ● Usually with tufted duck or pochard.

PMH 61; HTV 46

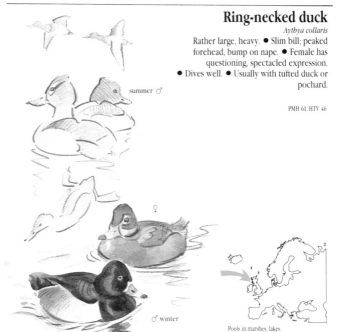

summer ♂

♀

♂ winter

Pools in marshes, lakes.

Tufted duck

Aythya fuligula

Medium-sized but round, big-headed, buoyant as a cork, lively. ● Dives frequently, rolling forwards slightly, bursting back on to surface with splash.
● Furtive if alarmed, sinks low and looks back over shoulder. ● Nape has drooping tuft on male, bump on female. ● Stands upright, rounded, legs well back. ● Quick, pattering, low take-off, flight fast, direct; barrel-bodied, wings look short. ● Flocks sweep low and bank round or climb steeply.

Growls, whistles
PMH 62: HTV 42

summer ♂

♀

winter ♂

Lakes, reservoirs, flooded pits.

Scaup

Aythya marila

Rather large, broad-beamed, solid and sedate.
● Big, broad bill, bulging cheeks on large, rounded head with smooth nape.
● Tail often cocked.
● Steady flight on broad wings. ● Large, quiet flocks, or occasional ones with tufted duck.

PMH 62, HTV 43; LWS 80

summer

winter ♂

♀

Sheltered coastal waters; estuaries.

Eider

Somateria mollissima
Big, heavy, lumbering,
placid and confiding.
- Wedge-shaped bill/head.
- Short tail often cocked.
- Swims low in water,
revels in rough seas.
- Dives with roll, flicking
wings half open. • Flight
heavy, always low, straight.
- Swims and flies in long,
irregular lines.

Cooing *aa-oo*
PMH 63; LWS 83

Broad, sandy coastal bays; rocky headlands.

King eider

Somateria spectabilis
Neater than eider, with
shorter bill, shorter,
rounder head and rounded
body with tiny 'sails'.
- Big, round shield and
head on adult male; female
has less gawky build than
eider; with open
expression.

PMH 63; LWS 261

year-old ♂

♀

winter ♂

♀

Coastal bays

44

Long-tailed duck

Clangula hyemalis
Small, neat, round-bodied.
● Bill squat on square or
domed head. ● Long,
pointed tail. ● Alert and
nervous, dives constantly
with wing-flick; bounces off
big waves. ● Auk-like
flight, but more agile,
twisting; silhouette well
balanced.

Yodelled *a-ahulee*
LWS 84

♂ summer

imm

summer ♀

winter ♀

winter ♂

Offshore, in sandy bays, estuaries.

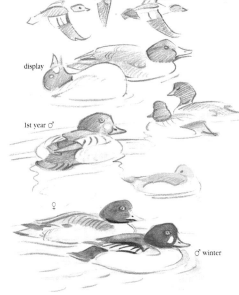

display

1st year ♂

♀

♂ winter

Goldeneye

Bucephala clangula
Quite large, bold-headed,
long- and deep-bodied.
● Female smaller, more
squat than male. ● Short,
triangular bill on high-
peaked head. ● Longish tail
flat on water or cocked
high when resting. ● Dives
constantly; suspicious,
quick to whirr away after
long, pattering take-off,
then fast, low flight with
wide, circling sweeps and
deep swoops back over
water; wings whistle loudly
in fast beats.

Growl; 'watch-winding' rattle
PMH 66; LWS 88

Coastal waters, lakes, reservoirs, upland
pools.

Common scoter

Melanitta nigra
Quite large. ● Shortish,
tapered bill on neat, long
head, thin neck, heavy
body. ● Frequently
hunched, round-backed;
pointed tail often cocked.
● Swims buoyantly, riding
the swell; flies in long lines
hugging the surface well
offshore.

winter ♂

Surf scoter

Melanitta perspicillata
Quite large, rather heavy;
shoe-bill on deep head.
● Female has more eider-
like profile. ● Flight low,
heavy, direct.

winter ♂

♀

Velvet scoter

Melanitta fusca
Large, bulky. ● Fine-tipped
but heavy bill on triangular
head. ● Long-backed body
profile, short tail sometimes
cocked. ● Flight low,
straight.

♀

winter ♂

Common scoter	Surf scoter	Velvet scoter

♂
♀

♂
♀

♂

♀

Musical, muted whistles
PMH 65; HTV 49

HTV 50

HTV 49; LWS 87

Large sandy coastal bays, shallow coastal
waters.

Sandy bays, estuaries.

Sandy bays, estuaries.

Red-breasted merganser

Mergus serrator

Large, skinny; male a dandy, long and elegant, swaggering, with roughly-crested head; females dull, smudgy.
● Thin, long bill almost upcurved; face with tight, smiling expression.
● Rides low in water; dives with ease. ● Flight fast, low; thin head and neck stretched out straight.

PMH 67; LWS 90

Broad, turbulent rivers; sea lochs, estuaries.

♀

winter ♂

Goosander

Mergus merganser

Large, cigar-shaped, weighty.
● Gorgeous male and smaller, clean female. ● Bill thick-based, hooked; forehead steep; crest even, drooped.
● Harsh expression. ● Rides low in water; horizontal on land. ● Dives with forward roll.
● Take-off needs long, splashing patter; flight then quick, direct, with blob head and neck outstretched.

LWS 91

♂

♀

winter ♂

Broad rivers; lakes and reservoirs.

Smew

Mergus albellus

Small, dapper, long-bodied. ● Small,
slim bill; male looks large-headed
with flared crown, drooped crest,
but female small-headed with steep
forehead. ● Buoyant, lively, nervous,
highly strung. ● Looks bigger,
heavy-bodied in fast, agile flight;
head small and stretched forward.

PMH 66

eclipse ♂

♂

♀

♂

Lakes, reservoirs, flooded pits.

Ruddy duck

Oxyura jamaicensis

Small, short; amusing, ball-shaped duck.
● Large, deep bill on big, bulbous head.
● Long, stiff tail flat or steeply cocked.
● Discreet, companionable. ● Flight
looks unlikely, but fast, whirring. ● In
pairs, parties or large flocks.

LWS 68

♂

♀

winter ♂

Reed-fringed lakes, reservoirs.

Osprey

LWS 102

Pandion haliaetus

Very large, somewhat gull-like with long, slim wings held in upward kink at wrist. ● Short tail, stubby head, large scaly feet. ● Flight active for so large a bird. ● Hovers heavily but expertly; dives headlong towards water, then tilts feet-first to enter with a splash. ● Sits upright on high perches, but inconspicuous near nest.

Large rivers, remote lakes, sandy coasts.

Black kite

Whinnying wail
PMH 69; HTV 52

Milvus migrans

Large, long-winged, rather long-tailed. ● Head and neck very short. ● Flight agile in chase or when snatching food in feet; otherwise slow, buoyant, with angled wings, elastic beats; wings flat or drooped at tips in glide, tail twisted, tilted, fanned, notched or sharply squared.

Wild marshes, wooded or rocky valleys.

Red kite

Wailing scream
PMH 69; LWS 94; HTV 52

Milvus milvus

Very large, attenuate bird of prey. ● Perches upright or stands horizontal on ground. ● Flight slow, agile, buoyant, with long, angled wings well forward; long, slim rear body and long, forked or notched triangular tail twisted, fanned and used as rudder. ● Glides with wings flat or angled downwards at wrist.

Wooded valleys, moorland, rocky hillsides.

White-tailed (sea) eagle

PMH 70

Huge. ● Massive bill on big head. ● Perches very upright.
● Broad, blunt wings held flat in glide like flying door; head
protrudes, tail very short. ● Wing-beats heavy, springy,
inelegant.

Coastal cliffs, fjords, lagoons

Golden eagle

PMH 77; LWS 102

Aquila chrysaetos

Huge yet elegant. ● Massive body and heavily feathered
thighs. ● Wings long, broad, held in V in soar. ● Tail longer
than head and neck. ● Long, slanting dives at great speed;
display deep switchback, wings curved back in rounded
bulge, tips close to tail. ● Glides perfectly attuned to winds;
circles in slow-motion unlike quickly wheeling buzzard.
● Often a distant speck, never on roadside pole.

Remote, extensive uplands; moors, crags.

dark

pale

Booted eagle

PMH 77

Hieraaetus pennatus

Rather large. ● Short hooked bill on rounded, protruding head; heavily feathered legs visible when perched. ● Flight elegant, with obvious round head and rather narrow, square tail; wings slimmer than buzzard's, slightly kite-like but straighter, tips deeply fingered or curved back to point; held flat in glide or soar and slightly pushed forward.

Forests, wooded ravines, scrubby slopes.

with snake

hovering

Short-toed eagle

PMH 71

Circaetus gallicus

Very large. ● Head big, cowled, rather owl-like; upright, stocky body; unfeathered legs. ● In flight, head looks large, round and protruding with striking pale eye; tail medium-length, often fanned. ● Wings broad and very long with outer half full and rounded but often angled back from wrist. ● Hovers with heavy, floppy, rowing beats; soars on flat or slightly raised wings.

Rocky, scrubby slopes, open woods, hot plains.

Marsh harrier

LWS 94

Circus aeruginosus

Large, with short, stubby head; long, rather straight wings; and rather long, narrow, square tail. Females heavy, broad; males lighter, slimmer. ● Flappy flight usually low; glides on wings raised in V; but soars well to an impressive height.

Reed-beds, swamps, coastal lagoons.

Hen harrier

Rapid chatter
LWS 96

Circus cyaneus

Large, but male light-weight, slim. ● Bulky, shapeless when perched. ● Wings rather straight or sharply angled back and untidily fingered at tips. ● Tail longish, usually held closed. ● Flight buoyant, low, steady but not as slow as it appears; wings in V in glides. ● Sudden pounce on to ground after prey; agile twisting chase of small bird.

Upland moors; reed-beds, dunes, pastures.

Montagu's harrier

LWS 96; HTV 54

Circus pygargus

Quite large, but slender, narrow-winged; female has outer wing long, curved back to point; male even slimmer, wings very long-tipped. ● Flight even more buoyant than other harriers.

Cereal crops, warm plains, reed-beds.

imm

ad

LWS 98

Goshawk
Accipiter gentilis

Large, sturdy; impression of muscular strength; female size of buzzard. ● Head protrudes more than sparrowhawk's; chest deeper; secondaries and tail broader, more rounded. ● Flight strong, with slower but powerful, deep wing-beats; short glides. ● Soars high, on flat wings.

Extensive or patchy forest, uplands.

♀

♂

Sparrowhawk
Accipiter nisus   PMH 73; LWS 98

Female quite big, male small, light-weight. ● Sharp expression, ever alert. ● Wings rather broad unless tips swept back to point; tail long, narrow. ● Dashing flight; low straight or from side to side of hedge or between trees. ● Several quick, winnowy beats, then wings snap into position for short, flat-winged glide. ● Soars with wings broadly spread, well forward.

Woods, parks, suburbia, farmland with hedges.

53

Honey buzzard

LWS 92

Pernis apivorus

Large and long-winged. ● Head and neck protrude, weak-looking. ● Tail long and narrow, or with bulging sides and rounded tip. ● Wings broad in centre, with narrower base and tip; active flight slow, wing-beats deep and soft, elastic/flappy; soars with wings flat or drooped.

Woodland tracts, heaths, parkland.

Buzzard

Shrill, screaming mew
PMH 74; LWS 100

Buteo buteo

Large; rather dumpy, heavy. ● Perches upright on trees, roadside poles (unlike eagle) or stands on ground. ● In flight, head short and broad; wings broad, rounded; tail often fanned; wing-beats slightly jerky, heavy, stiff. ● Soars with wings held up in shallow V, showing well-patterned undersides unlike eagle.

Wooded hills and valleys; crags, forest.

Rough-legged buzzard

LWS 101

Buteo lagopus

Very large; a class up on buzzard with long wings and long, broad tail; more flexible wing action recalls honey buzzard. ● Hovers frequently (as do some buzzards); hunts open country like huge harrier.

Moors; coastal fields, marshes, dunes.

Egyptian vulture

PMH 70

Neophron percnopterus

Large; scruffy, inelegant on ground. ● Thin bill and bare face give peevish expression; head has spiky crest. ● In flight; gains supreme elegance of form and action, with small, narrow head, rather narrow, pointed tail. ● Wings very long, broad, flat, deeply fingered or angled back and held closed to a point. ● Long, graceful glides, occasional deep down-beat.

Crags, ravines; village tips; forest clearings.

Black vulture

PMH 71

Aegypius monachus

Huge; very bulky, rather upright, with large, square head. ● Flight magnificent; head and tail very short and tail slightly wedge-shaped. ● Wings extremely long and broad, very heavy, angular, with rather straight trailing edge; deeply fingered. ● Soars with wings flat, glides with tips drooped; occasional slow, deep down-beat.

Forested hills, cliffs, high peaks.

Griffon vulture

PMH 71

Gyps fulvus

Huge. ● Smallish, rounded head on upright or sloping body. ● Flight splendid, with short head, very short tail, but immense wings. ● Trailing edge somewhat S-curved, tips warp upwards and whole wings held in slight V, giving variety of shapes from pointed to broadly-rounded and deep-fingered as bird circles. ● Wing-beats deep, laborious.

Crags, deep ravines, scrubby hillsides.

Kestrel *Falco tinnunculus*

Medium-sized; round-shouldered when perched. ● Upright or angled, but long tail hangs down. ● Sits for long periods; takes wing with sideways drop from perch. ● Flight flappy, with shallow, quick beats; shape changes to long and thin; tail straight and narrow or broadly fanned during accomplished hover with quivering wings, stationary head.

Lesser kestrel *Falco naumanni*

Rather small, slim. ● Rounded or chunky head on tapered, chesty body; long tail and wing tips. ● Flight quick, with stiffish, flappy, rather shallow wing-beats. ● Hovers like kestrel. ● Tail often has central feathers protruding, especially on male.

Merlin *Falco columbarius*

Small, dashing. ● Often perches, hunched on ground or low post. ● Wings broad-based, tapering to short, sharp point. ● Flight quick, level, low, with few glides; wing-beats shallow, flickering; when closing on prey uses slanting dive with wings partly closed, tips flickering, before final breathless, furious, twisting chase.

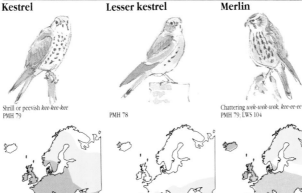

Kestrel	Lesser kestrel	Merlin
Shrill or peevish *kee-kee-kee* PMH 79	PMH 78	Chattering *wek-wek-wek, kee-ee-ee* PMH 79; LWS 104
Open space, farmland; cliffs, quarries, cities.	Ruins, big buildings; open plains and slopes.	Uplands moors; coastal heath, dunes, marshes.

Hobby *Falco subbuteo*
PMH 80; HTV 62

Quite large but light-weight, beautiful,
streamlined. ● Slender; short, tapered tail.
● Wings long, tapering, smoothly curved or
angled back. ● Swift-like or anchor
silhouettes frequent. ● Slow, sweeping glides
and stalls, catching insects in feet, or fast
patrolling with sudden dashes; or long, direct
stoop with flicks of almost closed wings after
bird.

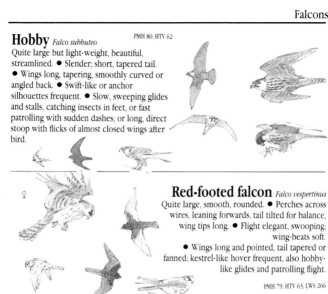

♀

Red-footed falcon *Falco vespertinus*

Quite large, smooth, rounded. ● Perches across
wires, leaning forwards, tail tilted for balance,
wing tips long. ● Flight elegant, swooping;
wing-beats soft.
● Wings long and pointed, tail tapered or
fanned; kestrel-like hover frequent, also hobby-
like glides and patrolling flight.

PMH 79; HTV 63; LWS 266

Eleonora's falcon
PMH 80; LWS 266

Falco eleonorae

Rather large. ● Long wings and tail.
● Flight shape like hobby but even
more rakish; longer wings sharply
pointed and angled; tail obviously
longer. ● Steady progress with
slow, elastic flaps and short,
wavering glides; hunting flight
quicker, also fast stoops and chases
after small birds.

dark

light

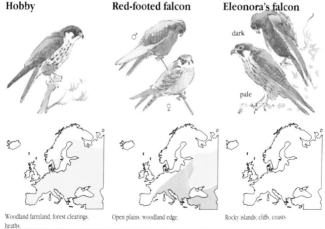

| Hobby | Red-footed falcon | Eleonora's falcon |

♂

dark

♀

pale

Woodland farmland, forest clearings, heaths.

Open plains, woodland edge.

Rocky islands, cliffs, coasts.

Gyrfalcon

Falco rusticolus

Very big, solid heavy-weight. ● Very broad body; broad, shortish tail. ● Wings broad-based, heavy, rather blunt. ● Flight powerful, low; direct flap-and-glide with accelerated, level chase after prey.

PMH 81; LWS 264

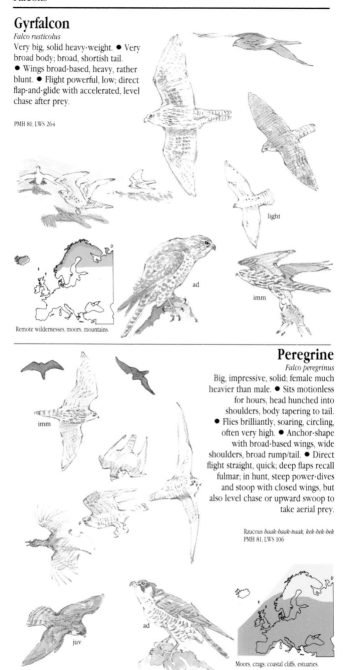

light

ad

imm

Remote wildernesses, moors, mountains.

Peregrine

Falco peregrinus

Big, impressive, solid; female much heavier than male. ● Sits motionless for hours, head hunched into shoulders, body tapering to tail. ● Flies brilliantly, soaring, circling, often very high. ● Anchor-shape with broad-based wings, wide shoulders, broad rump/tail. ● Direct flight straight, quick; deep flaps recall fulmar; in hunt, steep power-dives and stoop with closed wings, but also level chase or upward swoop to take aerial prey.

Raucous *baak-baak-baak, kek-kek-kek*
PMH 81; LWS 106

imm

juv

ad

Moors, crags, coastal cliffs, estuaries.

Capercaillie

Tetrao urogallus

Cock huge, like turkey, with bristling beard, drooped wings, fanned tail in display. ● Otherwise walks in horizontal crouch, tail long and closed. ● Smaller hen more crouched still, neck thrust low and forwards if suspicious. ● Often in treetops. ● Flies up with crashing wings, tail fanned, broadly rounded. ● Goes far off with long glides through clearings.

PMH 84

display

Extensive pine-woods, heathery clearings.

Black grouse

Tetrao tetrix

Big; rounded, cock with small head, lyre-shaped tail.
● Struts like rooster or crouches in heather.
● Often in dense trees. ● Smaller hen dumpy but with longish tail.
● Flight strong, often high and prolonged, with quick wing-beats, head well forwards and long rear body giving cross shape.

display

Bubbling croon; sneeze
PMH 83

Moorland edge, birch- and pine-woods, damp fields.

Ptarmigan
Lagopus mutus

Rotund. ● Short, stout bill on round head, thin neck. ● Body hump-backed, often crouched; short, fully-feathered legs. ● Walks freely rather than flies if disturbed, but display flight rises steeply, then long glide after 'stall'.

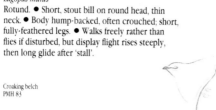

Croaking belch
PMH 83

winter

spring ♂

spring ♀

autumn ♂

High, bare, rocky plateaux, lower in north.

Red grouse
Lagopus lagopus

Rounded, chicken-like. ● Round head on rather slender neck, often withdrawn. ● Hump-backed when crouched, with heavy body. ● Short legs. ● Flies low, fast, with rapid bursts of stiff down-beats, short glides; neck outstretched.

Startling *cr-rr-rra-rra-go-bak go-bak-bak*
PMH 82

♂

♀

Heather moor, uplands with heather.

Red-legged partridge

Alectoris rufa
Rather large; rounded, with small head withdrawn into shoulders or stretched erect. ● Bulky, broad body, very short legs. ● Squats and shuffles, but runs fast if disturbed; flies if hard-pressed, with rapid beats of stiff, fingered wings.

Chuffing *chuk-chuk-chukarr*
LWS 112 (beware chukar hybrids)

ad ♂

imm

ad ♂

Grey partridge

Perdix perdix
Medium-sized. ● Small head often held up; body rather round and bulky; short tail depressed. ● Short legs, but nimble gait. ● Flies easily, with sudden take-off into low flight and glides between bursts of stiff wing-beats.

kee-rrit, k-vit-vit-vit
PMH 85

♀

Quail

Coturnix coturnix
Very small. ● Small, neat head; short, thin neck; rather rounded or oval-shaped body. ● Slips through vegetation with ease. ● Flies only if very hard-pressed, then goes away low and fast; wings rather slender and longer than partridge's; snipe-like flurry as it drops out of sight.

Liquid *quic-wic-ic*
PMH 86; LWS 112

ad ♂

Red-legged partridge **Grey partridge** **Quail**

Warm, rocky slopes, crops, dry cereal fields.

Meadows, cereals, dunes.

Cereals, meadows.

Pheasant

Phasianus colchicus

Large; cock unmistakable, with small,
erect head, bulbous body, long spiky tail,
longish legs. ● Smaller female rounder,
with neat head on slim neck, pointed tail.
Slow forward walk with high, dainty
steps. ● Flight a sudden burst – full-
speed from standstill – then long glide
down to land on the run. ● Beware
flying juveniles only half-grown.

Startling *korr-kok*
PMH 86

ad ♂

♀

Woods, pastures, marshes.

Golden pheasant

Chrysolophus pictus

Tall, slim, long-legged pheasant, with
arched, droop-tipped tail. ● Male has
broad, dense shawl over neck; female
tighter-feathered, neat and elegant.
● Flight rare, but sudden fast dash to
cover on foot usual.

Harsh shrieking crow
LWS 114

ad ♂

♀

ad ♂

Dense woods with rhododendrum or
conifers. England

Water rail

Rallus aquaticus

Small; from side, shows deep-bodied, tilt-tailed, forward-leaning bird with long bill, strong legs; from behind, bird appears flattened into thin cut-out .
● Usual walk slow, dainty, picking way through waterside plants with rhythmic steps, flicking raised tail and bobbing head. ● Flight low, weak but quick, with head raised, legs trailed; fluttery collapse into cover.

Pig-like squeal
LWS 116

ad

Dense reed-beds, swampy ditches, alder thickets.

Corncrake

Crex crex

Rather small, oval, slim-bodied; raises head on slender neck to call or look out from tall grasses. ● Flies up underfoot; untidy, with trailing legs and flappy, rounded wings, soon retreating into cover. ● Usually a mysterious voice.

crek-crek
PMH 89

ad

ad

Hay meadows, iris beds.

63

Spotted crake

Porzana porzana

Small, rotund, but slim-bodied from front
or rear. ● Round head and short, stout
bill. ● Scampers over mud or steps
slowly and deliberately through
waterside plants. ● Bobs head and flicks
tail. ● Flight weak but quick, with
fluttering wing-beats, dropping back into
cover in untidy flurry.

PMH 88. FBI 231

Sedge- and reed-beds, swamps.

ad

Little crake

Porzana parva

Very small, rounded, but long wing
points and tail. ● Tail often cocked, head
slung low; short bill. ● Slow, jerky walk;
quick, short flight or pattering run into
cover.

PMH 88. FBI 231

ad

Sedge- and reed-beds, ditches.

Moorhen

Gallinula chloropus

Elegant, high-stepping, round-bodied,
with tail often cocked. ● Bobs head in
time with rhythmic steps, flirts tail; toes
long but refined. ● Swims with springy
bobbing of head and jerked tail.
● Sudden pattering dash to cover with
wings high and fluttered over water, or
crouched run over land.

kruuk
PMH 89

Ponds, lakes, riversides, wet meadows.

Coot

Fulica atra

Quite large, rounded, short-tailed, round-headed.
● On land, upright, with big, clumsy feet. ● On
water, long, rounded back with tail low, not
cocked. ● Often dives, sometimes with forward
leap; may reappear on surface tail-first. ● Flies
heavily, with no manoeuvrability, legs trailed
(except in cold), wings flapped with much effort.

Kit, krrik
PMH 90

Pools, large lakes, reservoirs, gravel pits.

Little bustard

Tetrax tetrax

Fairly large, long-legged and rather long-necked, but often crouched out of sight.
● Steady, easy walk. ● Flies fast with neck outstretched; speed, whirring wings and large areas of white recall unusual pigeon or duck.

PMH 92

ad ♂

♀

Cereal fields, grassy plains.

Great bustard

Otis tarda

Huge; wary, aloof, elegant but very heavy bird. ● Large head and bill on slim neck.
● Strong legs give long-striding walk.
● Flight powerful, males especially heavy and broad-winged, females lighter, goose-like.

PMH 92

display ♂

♂

ad ♂

♀

Vast cereal fields, remote pastures.

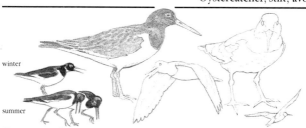

winter

summer

Oystercatcher *Haematopus ostralegus*

Large, heavy, short-legged. ● Plodding walk, pausing to probe/prod with strong bill held vertically; also short-stepping run. ● Head hunched at rest, raised in alarm, but body remains bulky. ● Flight strong, level and direct, on rather broad wings; deep, flappy or rather stiff beats. ● Feeds in loose groups, rests in tight flocks, which arrive at roost in noisy, crowding rush.

Piping *kleep-kleep*
PMH 93

Estuaries, mussel beds; grassy upland fields.

ads

♂

♀

1st summer

Noisy *kyik-kyik-kyik*
LWS 272

Black-winged stilt

Himantopus himantopus

High-standing, slim-bodied, pointed at rear. ● Enormously long legs, trailed in flight. ● Easy, quick walk or wobbling run, tipping forwards to feed; wades deeply, then picking from surface. ● Flight fast, with triangular, flexible wings angled at carpal joint. ● Bobs and extends neck in alarm.

Lagoons, salt pans, marshes.

juv

Avocet

Recurvirostra avosetta

Liquid *klute*
PMH 93

Tall, slim but deep-bodied. ● Long legs always evident, even in flight. ● Elegant, brisk walk and short runs. ● Flight fast, direct, with continuous fast, stiff beats of slightly-too-short wings. ● Wades deeply and swims, feeding with sideways sweep of bill.

Shallow, muddy, coastal lagoons, estuaries.

Golden plover *Pluvialis apricaria*

Round, small-headed, rather short-legged. ● Bill short with blunt tip.
● Hunched, round-shouldered, but head raised if wary. ● Runs then stops with head up, back sloping.
● Flocks often tight, well co-ordinated. ● Flight quick, just outpacing lapwings and separating out; wings pointed, flickering with regular wing-beats. ● Flocks pour in to land.

Piping *pyoo*; mournful *tloo*
PMH 97; LWS 124; HTV 67

juv

winter ad

Grey plover *Pluvialis squatarola*

Robust, bulky-bodied, quite long-legged. ● Bill rather thick and swollen. ● Dejected, hunched, slow-moving shape often looks heavy at long range. ● Walk, pause, tilt-over feeding action; wades. ● Flight swift, direct with momentum.

Whistled *tlee-oo-ee*
LWS 125; HTV 67

Lapwing *Vanellus vanellus*

Nasal *peer-wit*
PMH 99

Long-bodied, rather short-legged and -necked, with typical plover stop-go-tilt forward action when feeding. ● Large flocks loosely spread, standing quietly, still for long periods. ● Flight flickering, twisting, tilting over sideways; in long-distance flights, steadier, with rhythmic, twinkling beats of very broad, rounded wings.
● Display flights crazy, out-of-control dives and swerves.

winter

juv

| Golden plover | Grey plover | Lapwing |

winter

winter

juv

northern

southern
summer

summer

♀

♂

spring/autumn

Upland moors; lowland grassy pastures.

Muddy estuaries.

Meadows, moors, agricultural land.

Dotterel

LWS 126

Charadrius morinellus

Compact, often very rounded at rest; more upright, slimmer, apparently longer-legged when active. ● Short, fine bill. ● Delicate carriage; even-paced, quick walk. ● Flight quick, migrants often in small, close groups which circle then skim low over ground before settling. ● Wing-beats quick; rear body and tail rather broad.

High, rocky, mossy plateaux.

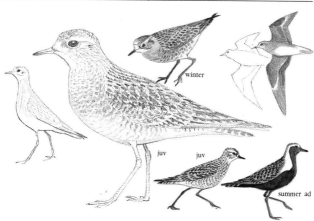

American golden plover

tchooik
HTV 67

Pluvialis dominica

Slight, small-headed, long-legged. ● Fine bill on squarish head, often raised on waisted neck. ● Rear body slim; wing tips tapered. ● Actions quick and light; flight fast, on narrow wings.

Open ground, sometimes with golden plovers; rare.

Little ringed plover *Charadrius dubius*

Abrupt *pew*
HTV 65

Small, slight; back flat and horizontal, wings and tail tapering; rather furtive-looking.
● Quick, lively actions, with short runs, forward tilts, many short flights. ● Flight fast, often gaining height, with rather short, narrow wings and tail.

Ringed plover *Charadrius hiaticula*

Rising *too-li*
PMH 95; HTV 65

Small, rounded, hunch-backed, rather long-bellied. ● Neckless, short-billed. ● Quick walk and short runs, with sudden stops and starts. ● Head raised or bobbed if alarmed. ● Flight low, quick, with regular flicking action, ending in glide then short run with raised wings.

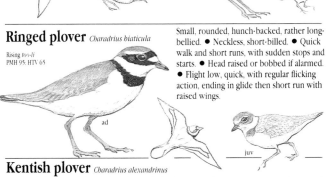

Kentish plover *Charadrius alexandrinus*

Small and slim, rounded and chick-like with thin legs set well back, or more upright, tapered stance. ● Fast, twinkling run, leaning far forwards. ● Flight quick and fluttering, landing with sudden flurry and dash along ground.

Sharp *pwit*
PMH 96; HTV 65

Little ringed plover　　**Ringed plover**　　**Kentish plover**

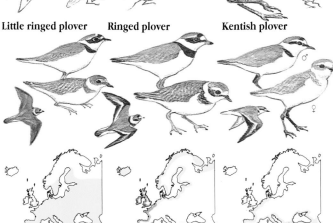

Sandy, shingly pools, lagoons, scrapes.　　Sandy coasts, dunes, pits, estuaries.　　Salt pans, sandy shores, lagoons.

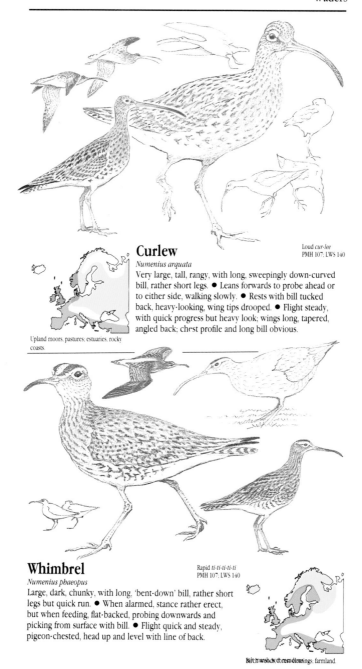

Curlew
Numenius arquata

Loud *cur-lee*
PMH 107; LWS 140

Very large, tall, rangy, with long, sweepingly down-curved
bill, rather short legs. ● Leans forwards to probe ahead or
to either side, walking slowly. ● Rests with bill tucked
back, heavy-looking, wing tips drooped. ● Flight steady,
with quick progress but heavy look; wings long, tapered,
angled back; chest profile and long bill obvious.

Upland moors, pastures; estuaries, rocky
coasts.

Whimbrel
Numenius phaeopus

Rapid *ti-ti-ti-ti-ti*
PMH 107; LWS 140

Large, dark, chunky, with long, 'bent-down' bill, rather short
legs but quick run. ● When alarmed, stance rather erect,
but when feeding, flat-backed, probing downwards and
picking from surface with bill. ● Flight quick and steady,
pigeon-chested, head up and level with line of back.

Salt marshes, breeding: farmland.

Black-tailed godwit
Limosa limosa

Large, tall, upstanding, long-legged and long-billed.
● Graceful, leggy walk, often wading deeply. ● Deep, vertical probes of tapered, straight bill. ● Small head and often noticeably long neck. ● Flight fast, with bill, body and trailing legs on same plane; loses height with twisting dive; display flight markedly aerobatic.

Nasal, lapwing-like *weeka-weeka*
LWS 138

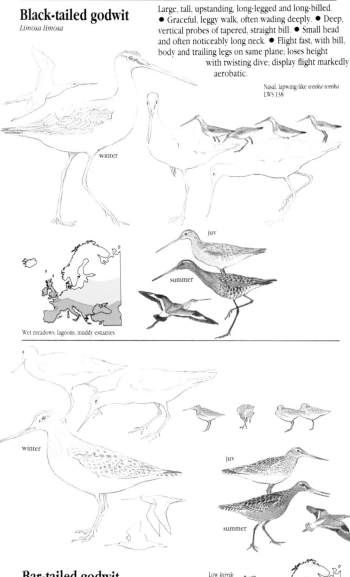

winter

juv

summer

Wet meadows; lagoons, muddy estuaries.

winter

juv

summer

Bar-tailed godwit
Limosa lapponica

Low *kirrik*
LWS 139

Rather large, dumpy, but without hunched effect of curlew; back often horizontal and body tapering to wing and tail tips. ● Bill over-long, slightly upswept; neck and legs rather short. ● Steady walk; short, clumsy runs with bill thrust forwards. ● Flight fast; flocks speedy, direct, descending with acrobatic, exciting corkscrew dives.

Muddy and sandy coasts; estuaries.

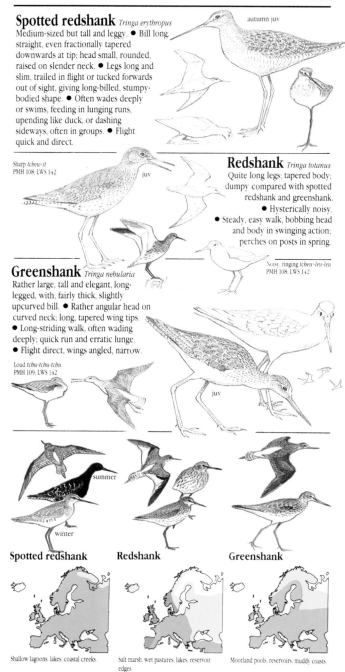

Spotted redshank *Tringa erythropus*

Medium-sized but tall and leggy. ● Bill long, straight, even fractionally tapered downwards at tip; head small, rounded, raised on slender neck. ● Legs long and slim, trailed in flight or tucked forwards out of sight, giving long-billed, stumpy-bodied shape. ● Often wades deeply or swims, feeding in lunging runs, upending like duck, or dashing sideways, often in groups. ● Flight quick and direct.

autumn juv

Sharp *tchew-it*
PMH 108; LWS 142

juv

Redshank *Tringa totanus*

Quite long legs; tapered body; dumpy compared with spotted redshank and greenshank.
● Hysterically noisy.
● Steady, easy walk, bobbing head and body in swinging action; perches on posts in spring.

Noisy, ringing *tchew-leu-leu*
PMH 108; LWS 142

Greenshank *Tringa nebularia*

Rather large, tall and elegant, long-legged, with, fairly thick, slightly upcurved bill. ● Rather angular head on curved neck; long, tapered wing tips.
● Long-striding walk, often wading deeply; quick run and erratic lunge.
● Flight direct, wings angled, narrow.

Loud *tchu-tchu-tchu*
PMH 109; LWS 142

juv

summer

winter

Spotted redshank

Redshank

Greenshank

Shallow lagoons, lakes, coastal creeks.

Salt marsh, wet pastures, lakes, reservoir edges.

Moorland pools, reservoirs, muddy coasts.

Lesser yellowlegs *Tringa flavipes*

Quite small, delicate, though deep-bodied, long-legged and slender-billed. ● Graceful walk and run, wading in shallows and probing or picking with markedly slender bill.
● Flight light and buoyant, wings rather broad, beats quite slow and elastic.

1st winter

Flat *tu tu*
LWS 280

Green sandpiper *Tringa ochropus*

Small but stout; small-headed but long-bodied. ● Legs and bill medium-short.
● Bobbing and swaying action of body exaggerated by longish tail. ● Flight often begins with sudden, noisy, towering escape, zigzagging to fair height before plummeting; wings look broad-based, but beats quick and relaxed.

Strident *tlooeet-weet-weet*
PMH 110; LWS 144

juv

Wood sandpiper *Tringa glareola*

Fairly small build, delicate and tapered but broad-bodied. ● Bill fine and straight; legs long and thin. ● Delicate walk, high-stepping when wading, picking from surface ahead or to side; stands with neck extended in alarm.
● Flight quick, agile; wing-beats fast and fluttery; rising with noisy, nervous calls; circling at a distance but not gaining much height before dropping.

Shrill *chiff-iff-iff*
PMH 111; LWS 144

juv

Lesser yellowlegs	**Green sandpiper**	**Wood sandpiper**
winter	winter	summer

spring/autumn

Vagrant from America

Sheltered lake edges; ditches, muddy creeks.

Muddy pools, lagoons.

Common sandpiper

Ringing *twee-wee-wee*
PMH 111

Actitis hypoleucos

Small, full-breasted, tapering to long tail. ● Bill short and straight; legs short. ● Slow, steady walk with frequent vertical swing of hind end; pauses to bob head and pump tail, or dashes in quick run. ● Flies out low over water if disturbed, landing after sudden twist. ● Wings longish, stiff, bowed and flickered in bursts of shallow beats; tail rounded.

Upland lakes, riversides, reservoirs, coasts.

Spotted sandpiper

Sharp *peet-weet-weet*
LWS 280; HTV 93

Actitis macularia

Small, like common, but at rest tail protrudes less beyond wing tips. ● Bill may be fractionally down-curved. ● Flight shares bowed, stiff, flickered wing-beats of common.

Muddy estuaries, pools; rare.

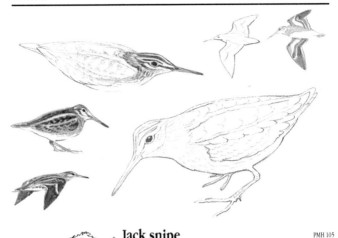

Jack snipe

PMH 105

Lymnocryptes minimus

Small, chubby snipe, with medium-length bill. ● Body bobs
as if on springs when feeding. ● Escape flight short, slow,
fluttering on broad wings, getting up to head height before
turning and dropping back out of sight. ● Often feeds in
same places as snipe, several together, but flies up one or
two at a time.

Flooded grassland, sedge-beds, weedy
mud.

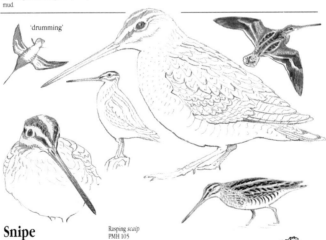

Snipe

Rasping *scaip*
PMH 105

Gallinago gallinago

Rather small, short-legged, compact wader with very long
bill and long, sloping forehead. ● Flies up with sudden,
zigzag dash, rising high and going far. ● Longer flights high,
quickly rolling from side to side showing long, sloping bill
and flicked, triangular wings. ● Display flight unique
switchback of steep rises and dives with vibrating wings and
outspread tail feathers. ● Gregarious; nearly always calls.

Oozy mud, wet fields, salt marsh, floods.

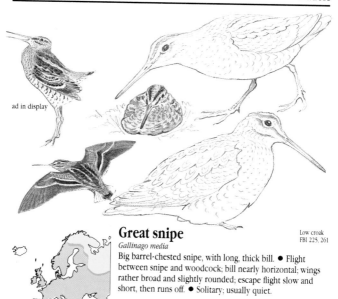

ad in display

Great snipe
Gallinago media

Low croak
FBI 225, 261

Big barrel-chested snipe, with long, thick bill. ● Flight between snipe and woodcock; bill nearly horizontal; wings rather broad and slightly rounded; escape flight slow and short, then runs off. ● Solitary; usually quiet.

Bracken, damp pastures, ditches.

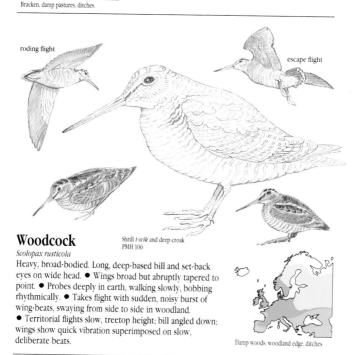

roding flight

escape flight

Woodcock
Scolopax rusticola

Shrill *t-wik* and deep croak
PMH 106

Heavy, broad-bodied. Long, deep-based bill and set-back eyes on wide head. ● Wings broad but abruptly tapered to point. ● Probes deeply in earth, walking slowly, bobbing rhythmically. ● Takes flight with sudden, noisy burst of wing-beats, swaying from side to side in woodland.
● Territorial flights slow, treetop height; bill angled down; wings show quick vibration superimposed on slow, deliberate beats.

Damp woods; woodland edge, ditches.

PMH 99; LWS 130

Muddy estuaries.

Knot

Calidris canutus

Medium-sized; chunky, yet rather long, short-legged, with straight, medium-length bill. ● Feeds in busy walk, probing quickly under its nose. ● Flight strong, wings rather long and tapered, body heavy, like plover. ● Very gregarious; feeds in tight swarms, advancing over mud; flies in dense 'smoky' clouds, with amazing manoeuvres.

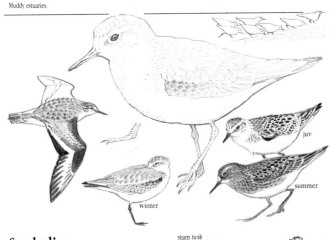

Sanderling

sharp *twik*
PMH 100; LWS 128

Calidris alba

Small but dumpy, with straight bill, rather short, twinkling legs. ● Strong plumage contrasts; obvious eye. ● Dashes along tide edge, chasing receding waves in fast, erratic runs; rests in dense, inactive flocks. ● Flight low, quick, direct but not aerobatic.

Sandy shores, estuaries.

spring/autumn

Little stint

Calidris minuta

Thin *tit-tit*
PMH 101; BB 77:293

Tiny, nippy, lively wader with short, straight bill, slim, medium-length legs; body rather round and dumpy; head neat, round. ● Picks from surface with quick nervy jabs, in quick walk, short runs. Flight fast, jinking, with quick wing-beats, instant manoeuvrability. ● Usually few at a time.

Muddy shore, lagoons, reservoir edges.

Temminck's stint

Calidris temminckii

Trilled *trr-r-r-ip*
PMH 101; BB 77:293

spring/autumn

Tiny, quiet, retiring; neat, round head and long, tapered body; rather short legs. ● Sandpiper-like bob at times; feeds with plodding walk, quick stabs. ● Escape flight fast, twisting and rising to impressive height. ● Usually alone.

Sheltered pools, muddy lake edges.

79

summer

juv

White-rumped sandpiper

Squeaky *jeet*
PMH 102; LWS 276

Calidris fuscicollis

Long, horizontal, tapering owing to long wing points; neat, compact at front, with shortish, straight bill. ● Feeding action between stint and dunlin. ● Flight quick on long, tapered wings.

Vagrant from North America; muddy pools.

with dunlin

Baird's sandpiper

Trilled *krreep*
LWS 276

Calidris bairdii

Small, compact, low and horizontal but elongated due to long, tapering wing tips. ● Short bill and legs. ● Steady walk or twinkling run. ● Flight reveals long, tapered wings.

Vagrant from North America; muddy pools.

summer

♀

juv

Pectoral sandpiper

Reedy *krreet*
LWS 130

Calidris melanotos

Quite small, head rather small; body tapered but rather broad. ● Very round when hunched, yet tall, long-necked if alert. ● Bill short, slightly down-curved. ● Slow feeding actions, probing and picking while standing or stepping forwards; crouches in hollows like snipe. ● Flight erratic, then light and loose with regular beats once under way.
● Loner.

Vagrant from North America; muddy pools.

Purple sandpiper

Low, sharp *weet-wit*
PMH 103; LWS 130

Calidris maritima

Rounded, dumpy, thick-necked; bill quite stout-based, tapered, slightly curved. ● Plain-faced but prominent eye. ● Lively, yet methodical feeder, probing in seaweeds, leaping aside to avoid waves or fluttering to adjacent rocks. ● Flight low and urgent, direct over long distances, settling with flutter. ● Often with turnstones.

Seaweedy, rocky coasts; strand lines.

Broad-billed sandpiper

Dry *tirrreek*
LWS 276

Limicola falcinellus

Small, neat, chunky, with thin bill with slight kink at tip; square head, short legs. ● Probes delicately with bill vertical; crouches if alarmed. ● Flight low, often for short distances. ● Unobtrusive.

Lagoons, estuaries.

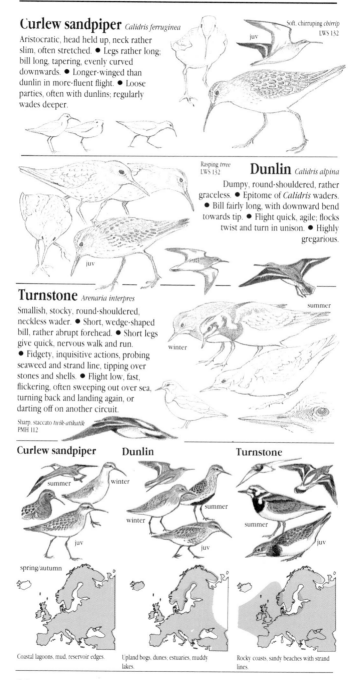

Curlew sandpiper *Calidris ferruginea*

Aristocratic, head held up, neck rather slim, often stretched. ● Legs rather long; bill long, tapering, evenly curved downwards. ● Longer-winged than dunlin in more-fluent flight. ● Loose parties, often with dunlins; regularly wades deeper.

Soft, chirruping *chirrip*
LWS 132

juv

Rasping *tiree*
LWS 132

Dunlin *Calidris alpina*

Dumpy, round-shouldered, rather graceless. ● Epitome of *Calidris* waders. ● Bill fairly long, with downward bend towards tip. ● Flight quick, agile; flocks twist and turn in unison. ● Highly gregarious.

juv

Turnstone *Arenaria interpres*

Smallish, stocky, round-shouldered, neckless wader. ● Short, wedge-shaped bill, rather abrupt forehead. ● Short legs give quick, nervous walk and run. ● Fidgety, inquisitive actions, probing seaweed and strand line, tipping over stones and shells. ● Flight low, fast, flickering, often sweeping out over sea, turning back and landing again, or darting off on another circuit.

summer

winter

Sharp, staccato *twik-atikatik*
PMH 112

Curlew sandpiper	Dunlin	Turnstone

summer · winter · juv

winter · summer · juv

summer · juv

spring/autumn

Coastal lagoons, mud, reservoir edges.

Upland bogs, dunes, estuaries, muddy lakes.

Rocky coasts, sandy beaches with strand lines.

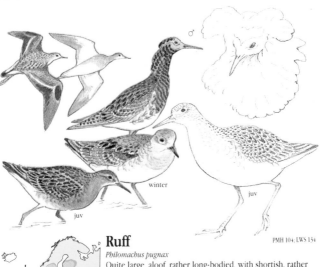

Ruff

PMH 104; LWS 134

Philomachus pugnax

Quite large, aloof, rather long-bodied, with shortish, rather thick, slightly curved bill on neat, round head. ● Neck often held up, when long but still quite thick. ● Feeds slowly, with steady, wandering walk. ● Flight noticeably lazy and floating owing to loose, slow action of long wings. ● Adult males noticeably larger than others. ● Often mixed with other waders but separates in flight.

Floods, lagoons, lakes, reservoirs.

Buff-breasted sandpiper

LWS 278; HTV 78

Tryngites subruficollis

Neat, rounded, with rather short, fine bill on small, round head. ● Longish legs give quick, easy run. ● Feeds with crouching forward lean, but high-stepping action. ● Flies off low, with sudden twists, on long wings

Short grass.

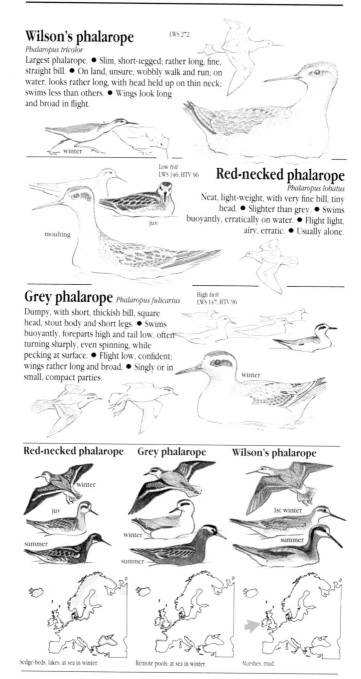

Wilson's phalarope

LWS 272

Phalaropus tricolor

Largest phalarope. ● Slim, short-legged; rather long, fine, straight bill. ● On land, unsure, wobbly walk and run; on water, looks rather long, with head held up on thin neck; swims less than others. ● Wings look long and broad in flight.

winter

Low *tuit*
LWS 146; HTV 96

juv

moulting

Red-necked phalarope

Phalaropus lobatus

Neat, light-weight, with very fine bill, tiny head. ● Slighter than grey. ● Swims buoyantly, erratically on water. ● Flight light, airy, erratic. ● Usually alone.

Grey phalarope *Phalaropus fulicarius*

High *tuit*
LWS 147; HTV 96

Dumpy, with short, thickish bill, square head, stout body and short legs. ● Swims buoyantly, foreparts high and tail low, often turning sharply, even spinning, while pecking at surface. ● Flight low, confident; wings rather long and broad. ● Singly or in small, compact parties.

winter

Red-necked phalarope

winter

juv

summer

Grey phalarope

winter

summer

Wilson's phalarope

1st winter

summer

Sedge-beds, lakes; at sea in winter.

Remote pools; at sea in winter.

Marshes, mud.

Stone curlew

Wailing *curlee*
PMH 94: LWS 120

Burhinus oedicnemus

Large, inconspicuous, like big plover. ● Pale base to short, stout bill more obvious than head/eye pattern. ● Round head, thin neck, heavy body; tapered wing tips, long tail. ● Stands erect, or squats; long-stepping walk. ● Flight strong, on long, tapered wings; tail trailing. ● Often just a wail in the night.

Flinty, chalky fields, rabbit-grazed pastures.

ad

juv

Tern-like *kirrikiki*
PMH 94: LWS 272

Collared (red-winged) pratincole

Glareola pratincola

Medium-sized, swallow-like form. ● Short-billed, short-legged, long-tailed. ● Stands with round head held up on short neck above full chest; body tapers into long tail/wing tips. ● In air, acrobatic, wings long, sharply pointed; tail held as point or with thin streamers spread in fork.
● Flocks feed in air in loose association.

Dried mud, lagoons, grassland.

85

ad

Great skua

PMH 115; LWS 148

Stercorarius skua

Large, solid, confident. ● Thick bill on small head; pot-belly looks heavy. ● Wings long, broad, pointed; tail short and wedge-shaped. ● Flight low over sea, or soaring over land; slow and ponderous before sudden acceleration into rapid, agile chase after large sea-birds.

Northern isles and mainland moors; sea.

winter

ad

ad

juv

Pomarine skua

LWS 148; BB 82:143

Stercorarius pomarinus

Large, menacing. ● Long, deep-chested but tapering profile, ending in broadly twisted tail streamers on breeding adults. ● Wings broad-based, long-armed, abruptly tapering to pointed tips. ● Flight between Arctic and great, at times gull-like. ● Agile but powerful. ● Chase after gulls and terns determined and prolonged.

Off coastal headlands, estuaries.

summer visitor, also autumn passage

Northern isles, moors; at sea, off coasts.

Arctic skua

LWS 150; BB 82:143

Stercorarius parasiticus

Elegant, sharp-winged, falcon-like pirate. ● Short bill, small head on broad, pot-bellied body, short legs. ● In flight, looks slim; wings long, flexible, often angled at wrist, pointed. ● Tapers to pointed tail projection on adults. ● Languid, low flight changes to sudden acceleration with deep, powerful wing-beats ending in dynamic chase, with loops, twists, dives.

Long-tailed skua

LWS 150; BB 82:143

Stercorarius longicaudus

Slender, slinky, light-weight. ● Wings long and slim, body tapers to long tail with very long, whippy streamers on adults. ● Flight easy, tern-like. ● Twisting, breathless chase less frequent than Arctic's; feeds on surface of sea.

autumn passage

Migrates off shore or along coasts.

Ivory gull *Pagophila eburnea*

Quite large. ● Round head; dumpy, pigeon-like body; short legs cloaked by belly feathers. ● Wings long, paddle-shaped, giving slightly stiff flight action.

imm

ad

Glaucous gull *Larus hyperboreus*

Big, aggressive, mean. ● Bill long, strong, hooked, on large head with small, glinting eye. ● Body big and heavy, looking long, with wing tips cloaking tail. ● Long, sturdy legs. ● Flight heavy, ponderous, like herring or slower.

year old

ad

Iceland gull *Larus glaucoides*

Large gull with short, squat bill, abrupt forehead, big eye in round head. ● Body rather heavy, sloping, with wing tips very long and drooped; legs short. ● Flight like herring gull but quicker, more expert; rather heavy-bodied but long-winged.

herring

ad

year old

Ivory gull

Glaucous gull

ad

imm

Iceland gull

ad

imm

PJG 138; PMH 122

PJG 141; LWS 160; HTV 123

PJG 151; LWS 160; HTV 123

Coasts.

Harbours, beaches, tips, reservoirs.

Coasts, tips, pastures, harbours.

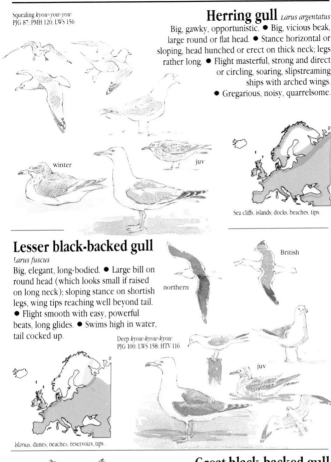

Squealing *kyow-yow-yow*
PJG 87; PMH 120; LWS 156

Herring gull *Larus argentatus*

Big, gawky, opportunistic. ● Big, vicious beak, large round or flat head. ● Stance horizontal or sloping, head hunched or erect on thick neck; legs rather long. ● Flight masterful, strong and direct or circling, soaring, slipstreaming ships with arched wings. ● Gregarious, noisy, quarrelsome.

winter

juv

Sea cliffs, islands; docks, beaches, tips.

Lesser black-backed gull

Larus fuscus

Big, elegant, long-bodied. ● Large bill on round head (which looks small if raised on long neck); sloping stance on shortish legs, wing tips reaching well beyond tail. ● Flight smooth with easy, powerful beats, long glides. ● Swims high in water, tail cocked up.

British

northern

Deep *kyow-kyow-kyow*
PJG 100; LWS 158; HTV 116

juv

Islands, dunes, beaches, reservoirs, tips.

Great black-backed gull

Larus marinus

Very big, mean bully, vulturine behaviour. ● Bill very heavy, hooked, on big, round head. ● Rather horizontal, very heavy body on long legs; long, broad, angled wings give powerful, padding flight action. ● Dominant.

heron

Very deep *yow-yow*
PJG 111; LWS 162; HTV 116

summer

Cliffs and stacks; tips, beaches, reservoirs.

89

Ring-billed gull *Larus delawarensis*

PJG 63; HTV 111

Quite large, upstanding, long-legged.
● Bill thick, parallel-edged as if slightly open, on rounded or flat-topped head; staring eye at close range. ● Quick, long-stepping walk. ● In flight, wings broader-based, tapered to sharper point, than common.

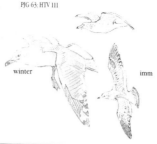

winter   imm

ring-billed   common

imm

winter

summer

PJG 39

Bonaparte's gull
Larus philadelphia

Small, light-weight, waif-like. ● Tiny bill on small head like little gull. ● Delicate body like black-headed, but legs shorter. ● Flight buoyant, bouncy, tern-like.

Mediterranean gull

PJG 58; PMH 116; LWS 152

Larus melanocephalus

Quite small, ghostly but aggressive; chunky, deep-chested. ● Bill thickish, blob-tipped, on square head. ● Head-up, chin-in, chest-out stance; longish legs set well forward, giving quick run, high-stepping walk. ● Flight elegant; wings rather straight and square, tail short.

summer

juv

winter

black-headed   Mediterranean   common

Ring-billed gull	Bonaparte's gull	Mediterranean gull

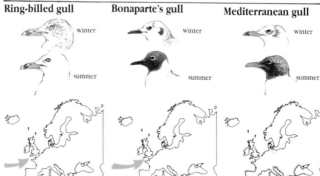

| winter | winter | winter |
| summer | summer | summer |

Breeds lochs, moorland; winters coasts, reservoirs, farmland.

Lakes, marshes, coastal lagoons, tips, fields.

Sandy, muddy beaches, estuaries.

Black-headed gull

Larus ridibundus

Rather small, lithe, agile, noisy entrepreneur. ● Slender, pointed bill on small, rounded head. ● Tapered body; longish legs give quick, pattering run. ● Flight light and airy, wings pointed, beats flickering or smooth. ● Arguing, scrapping, chasing flocks forage very widely.

Scolding *kwarrr*
PMH 118; LWS 154

winter

juv

summer

Lakes, marshes, coastal lagoons; tips, fields.

Common gull

Larus canus

Medium-sized, neat and elegant, meek-looking. ● Neat, smallish bill; beady eye in round head. ● Long-bodied, wing tips well beyond tail; easy walk over short grass, beaches. ● Flight easy, sweeping, fluent, less soaring/gliding than herring; wings slightly blunted. ● Squealing, squabbling, gregarious.

Squealing, shrill *keeya-ya-ya*
PJG 51; HTV 112

winter

summer

winter

Rocky coasts, moors; fields, beaches, lakes.

91

Kittiwake *Rissa tridactyla*

Quite small, neat, tapered. ● Small, curved bill on round head with gentle expression. ● Long, narrow wing tips cross over tail at rest; very short legs give sit-back-on-tail effect. ● Flight graceful, with angled, tapered wings; in calm, steady flaps, rather light and springy; in wind, marked shearing, rising and falling in long, banking bounds in gale. Head/neck protrude, as prominent as short, notched tail.

ad

juv

juv

summer

Sabine's gull

Larus sabini

Rather small, elegant but slightly fragile. ● Short, stout bill on small, neat, round head; somewhat pigeon-like body at rest. ● Forked or notched tail. ● Flight light or bounding, shearing in strong wind.

Little gull *Larus minutus*

Tiny, neat and cute. ● Short, slim, spiky beak set low on small round head; tiny dark eye. ● Dumpy body but long wings, short little legs. ● Flight steady, easy, direct or swooping with banking turns, dips and dives. ● Groups often soar up then stream down again line astern. ● Floats like a cork.

winter

summer

1st winter

juv

Kittiwake	Sabine's gull	Little gull

breeding

Nasal *kitti-ya-ake*
PJG 134; LWS 162

breeding

PJG 129; LWS 154

breeding

PMH 117; PJG 119; LWS 152

also spring/autumn

Sea cliffs; offshore waters, harbours.

Offshore waters.

Marshes, lakes and reservoirs, harbours.

White-winged black tern *Chlidonias leucopterus*

Small, rather dumpy.
● Shortish, spiky bill, round head; long legs give high stance.
● Flight rather flat and straight with few side-sweeps, less buoyant than black; wings slightly blunted, tail notched.

summer

juv

winter

Whiskered tern *Chlidonias hybridus*

Rather heavy, recalls sea tern. ● Bill heavy and long, head flattish. ● Wings broad-based but long and pointed; flight dipping and swooping, but long, straight patrolling flights over water/wet marsh.

summer

juv

Black tern *Chlidonias niger*

Neat, elegant, light-weight.
● Long, slender bill, rounded head. ● Short legs give low, long stance. ● Flight dipping, swooping, frequent side-sweeps and rolls; wings tapered to point, beat loosely.

winter

summer

juv

juv

White-winged black tern	Whiskered tern	Black tern

summer ad

PMH 126; LWS 286; FBI 6

summer ad

PMH 125; LWS 286; FBI 6

summer ad

Squeaky *keek*
PMH 126; LWS 166; FBI 6

Reedy pools, marshes, reservoirs.

Marshes, pools, lakes.

Floods, marshes, lakes and reservoirs.

Gull-billed tern

Gelochelidon nilotica
Rather large, heavy upfront.
● Thick, short, pointed bill on
round head and thick neck. ● Deep-
bodied, long-legged with gull-like
stance. ● Flight lazy but elegant, on
long, tapered wings; tail notched.
● Sweeps over marshy ground,
dipping and stalling.

Harsh *ka-buk*
HTV 128

summer

winter

Shallow lagoons, coastal marshes, wet
fields.

Sandwich tern

Sterna sandvicensis
Long, sharp-billed, long-faced, aggressive
and noisy. ● Bill long, slim, sharp on
largish head with spiky crest at nape; tail
rarely striking. ● Ghostly. ● Flight
strong and fast, often quite high; wings
very long, angled, tapered; dives into sea
after little or no hover, with loud smack
and big splash.

Rasping, sharp *kierrink*
PMH 123; HTV 128

autumn

spring

Lagoons, dunes, inshore waters.

Nasal, scolding *kee-yah*
PMH 124; LWS 165; HTV 133

Common tern
Sterna hirundo

Medium-sized, long-winged, long-tailed.
● Long, rather stout bill and longish,
flattish head. ● Long tail streamers on
adults reach wing tips at rest. ● Flight
direct, quick, rather stable, with
head/neck protruding, inner part of wing
rather long. ● Turns on sighting prey, to
hover and dive, or dives at angle from
low altitude.

juv

Rocky islands, dunes, beaches, lakes, rivers.

Arctic tern *Sterna paradisaea*

High *keeah*
LWS 164; HTV 133

Medium-sized, beautiful, graceful. ● Spiky bill on
rather short, rounded head. ● Long tail streamers
exceed tail length. ● Very short legs. ● In flight head/
neck short, thick; wings long, angled, short-armed, but
with long, tapered tips. ● Flight light and airy, body
rises/falls. ● Dives from height, with 'stepped' series
of hovers in vertical descent

juv

Rocky islands, dunes, inshore waters.

tchuit and croak
HTV 133

Roseate tern *Sterna dougallii*

Medium-sized. ● Long, spiky bill on
longish, domed head; stance upright, like
Sandwich. ● Long legs; very long tail
streamers exceed tail length. ● Flight
direct, rather quick, on shortish, blunt
wings with quick beats.
● Forages widely, plunging in
power dive from great height with
little or no hover, then moving far off
before next dive.

Rocky islands with vegetation; coasts.

Little tern

Sterna albifrons

Tiny, rapid, hurried. ● Excitable and irritable; pointed bill on large head. ● Flight fast with whirring wings; hover steeply angled, fast, before stinging dive into waves, often very close to beach.

Rapid *kikikik*
PMH 125; LWS 166

juv

with ringed plover

Sand and shingle beaches, coastal lagoons.

Caspian tern

Sterna caspia

Very big and heavy, gull-like. ● Stout, dagger bill on large, deep head; bulky neck and chest, long legs, horizontal stance. ● Flight strong, direct on long, angled wings. ● Almost gannet-like.

Harsh *krraa*
PMH 123; LWS 284

autumn

spring

Beaches, lagoons, islands.

Little auk

Alle alle

Small, squat. ● Tiny bill on frog-like face;
thick neck often retracted. ● On water
looks dumpy but buoyant, with short,
sometimes cocked, tail. ● Dives from
surface. ● Flight fast, low, direct with
whirring wings. ● Passes headlands in
small numbers, or swims offshore usually
alone.

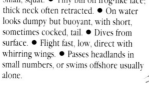

crop full

PMH 128

winter

Inshore and offshore waters.

summer   breeding

Puffin

Fratercula arctica

Small, stocky, barrel-bodied. ● In
summer, very large, triangular bill follows
forehead profile, on rounded head; in
winter, bill a smaller, more elongated
triangle. ● Swaggering, upright walk on
land; buoyant on water with frequent
dives with forward roll and splash.
● Flight quick, with too-heavy body and
whirring, narrow wings; can also hang-
glide in updraughts at cliff edge.
● Exceptionally gregarious.

PMH 128

juv

Islands, sea cliffs; offshore waters.

Guillemot *Uria aalge*

winter

Elegant, slim auk. ● Bill long and tapered; pointed face to triangular head; tail short and square. ● On land, stands upright, resting on tarsi, with uncomfortable shuffle; on water, looks long with upright neck; often stands on tail to flap wings. ● Flight fast and straight.

PMH 126

Sea cliffs; offshore waters.

Razorbill

Alca torda

Large, stocky auk with square-tipped, deep, blade-like bill, flat forehead, square head and thick neck. ● Upright on land, squatting on tarsi; on water, chunky head withdrawn, pointed tail often cocked. ● Frequent dives from surface. ● Flight fast and direct, wings whirring.

winter

PMH 127

Sea cliffs; inshore and offshore waters.

Black guillemot *Cepphus grylle*

Smallish, rounded auk. ● Slender bill, rounded head and rather rotund body. ● Angled or upright stance on land; on water, bounces like a cork. ● Flight very low over water, fast, with blur of wings. ● Ones and twos.

winter

PMH 127; LWS 170

Rocky coasts; islands, sheltered firths.

98

Rock dove/feral pigeon

Rolling croon *oo-roo-coo*
PMH 130

Columba livia

Large, rather heavy. ● Small bill with large basal bulge on birds from domestic stock. ● Round head, slender neck; big, rounded chest. ● Short, stout legs;, easy, waddling walk; with jerking head; pecks rapidly with rhythmic action. ● Flight fast, swooping, with clattering escape; dizzy glides; downward spirals with wings raised in V. ● Racers have more protruding head, swept-back wings.

Cliffs, coastal fields; feral birds anywhere.

Stock dove

Deep, rhythmic *oo-ro*
PMH 130; LWS 172

Columba oenas

Rather large, rotund. ● Round head, slim neck, dumpy body. ● In flight, head rounder, wings and tail shorter than woodpigeon. ● Clattering escape; flocks in scores where common.

Old woods, parks; farmland with trees.

Woodpigeon

Restful *ooo-coo-coo coo-cu*
PMH 130

Columba palumbus

Very large pigeon; small, round head, broad shoulders, long tail. ● Low-slung, slow, waddling walk. ● Escape sudden, very fast, crashing through undergrowth or clattering into clear air. ● Wings and tail long; head small; chest deeply rounded in flight. ● Glides and flaps on slight switchback track, or flies high, direct and steady with continuous beats. ● Gregarious.

Woods, hedges, farmland and parks.

Turtle dove

Soothing, rolling *prrr-urr*
PMH 131

Streptopelia turtur

Small, slender dove; neat, round head, long wings and broad tail. ● Often perches sloping across wire. ● Quick, steep escape from ground; direct flight easy, swift, tilting from side to side during short glides; wings pointed, beat with backward flicks. ● Lands in flurry with fanned tail.

Tall hedges; woodland edge; stubble fields.

Collared dove

Abrupt *cu-coo-cuk*
PMH 131

Streptopelia decaocto

Medium-sized; small, round head bobs rhythmically during neat, mincing walk. ● Flight direct, quite quick; small, round head protrudes; wings rather bowed and rounded; tail long, fairly broad but held closed, tapered.

Parks, gardens, farmsteads.

juv

Cuckoo

Familiar *cu-coo*
PMH 132; LWS 174

Cuculus canorus

Fairly large, elongated, looks prehistoric. ● Pointed wings often drooped beside long, fanned, swivelling tail.
● Narrow head raised, questioning expression. ● Flight low, rolling, unstable; quick, shallow down-beats look tiring.
● More heard than seen.

Moors, marshes, woodland edge, farmland.

Yellow-billed cuckoo

LWS 288

Coccyzus americanus

Smaller than cuckoo.● Thin bill and head; slim body; longish tail like cuckoo, but wings more blunt; tail fanned, strikingly marked beneath. ● Flight more shooting, less unstable than cuckoo.

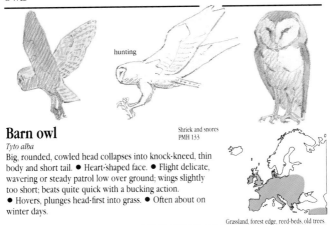

Barn owl

Shriek and snores
PMH 133

Tyto alba

Big, rounded, cowled head collapses into knock-kneed, thin body and short tail. ● Heart-shaped face. ● Flight delicate, wavering or steady patrol low over ground; wings slightly too short; beats quite quick with a bucking action.
● Hovers, plunges head-first into grass. ● Often about on winter days.

Grassland, forest edge, reed-beds, old trees.

Snowy owl

PMH 134

Nyctea scandiaca

Huge, regal; big, round or flattened head and heavy body form blob on massive feathery feet. ● Cat-like face. ● In flight, long-winged and impressive; wing-beats slow downwards, quick upwards. ● Active by day.

Remote moors, tundra.

Tawny owl

Wavering hoot; sharp *ke-wick*
PMH 135

Strix aluco

Big with heavy round head, short tail out of balance.
● Squat and hunched at rest or slim and upright in alarm.
● Flight quick, short, heavy, direct and level; wings broad and rounded. ● Perches in trees. ● Nocturnal except in freeze.

Woods, parks and farmland with old trees.

Long-eared owl

Deep moaning *coo*
PMH 136

Asio otus

Big, usually slender owl; squat; at rest face like cat, becomes V-shaped when asleep; upright, attenuated in alarm, when may raise ear tufts. ● In trees and thickets, only over open ground at night. ● Flight easy, rather quick, on long wings.

Conifers, old thickets, willows, open ground.

Short-eared owl

Barking *bu-bu-bu*
PMH 137

Asio flammeus

Big and 'loose' owl; ears rarely show. ● Settles on ground or post in sloping pose; fierce face with smouldering eye. ● Low, wavering, gliding patrols on long, fairly slim wings over open spaces, often in daylight.

Heather moor, marshes, plantations, dunes.

Tengmalm's owl

Aegolius funereus

PMH 137

Small, broad-headed; continual surprised, wide-eyed
expression owing to raised brows. ● Quick, flurried, level
flight. ● Strictly woodland; skulks.

Dense forest.

Little owl

Athene noctua

Shrill *kwee-oo*
PMH 135

Small, dumpy, curious. ● Fierce, flat-browed, frowning face.
● Bobs and twists head. ● Round ball with feet, stretches
up into quite tall bird. ● Flight quick, flappy, with deep,
bounding undulations. ● Often out (but inactive) by day.

Farmland with old trees; parks, ruins, crags.

Scops owl

Otus scops

Repeated *pieu; pieu*
PMH 133

Very small; usually quite slim; upright but dumpier when
relaxed. ● Triangular, flat-topped head with raised
'corners'. ● Short flights whirring, dipping. ● Disembodied
voice after dark.

Wooded gardens, parks, villages.

Nightjar

Caprimulgus europaeus

Prolonged rapid, hollow churr
PMH 137

Mysterious, eerie. ● Quite large, lengthy. ● Long head, 'no beak or feet'. ● Stretches out on perch or ground. ● Flight silent, wheeling, buoyant; shows long wing and tail of almost equal size; tail often broadly fanned. ● Glides with wings in deep V; hovers, dips and side-slips erratically with mechanical beats.

Heaths, bush places, woodland edge.

Swift

Apus apus

Shrill scream
PMH 138

Larger than swallow; flying anchor shape. ● Never perches on wires or roofs. ● Short, blunt head; slender 'cigar' body with long rear half tapering to pointed or forked tail; wings scythe-shaped, stiff, flickered rapidly. ● Glides slowly, often very high, with wings depressed or flat. ● Frequent madcap, round-the-houses chases.

Open air, over villages, farms, lakes.

Alpine swift

Apus melba

Rapid trill
PMH 139

Big swift, impressive, cleaves the air. ● Relaxed, yet powerful, direct flight on long, scimitar wings, often rolling gently from side to side. ● Sudden fast dives and swoops; erratic twists and turns.

Craggy valleys; cliffs, open space

105

Kingfisher

Alcedo atthis

Shrill *chi-kee*
PMH 140

Rather small, squat. ● Heavy, long bill and large head, tubby body, but tiny feet and tail. ● Perches upright, with bill/head inclined forwards or down, tail depressed. ● Dives headlong or belly-flops into water from perch or after hover. ● Flies fast, low; direct, whirring wings.

Lakes, rivers, marshes, sea coast in winter.

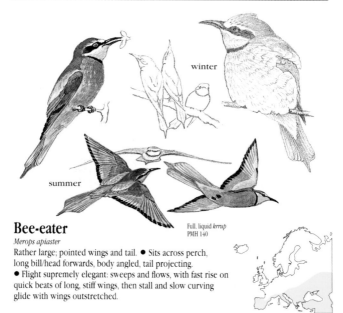

winter

summer

Bee-eater

Full, liquid *krrup*
PMH 140

Merops apiaster

Rather large; pointed wings and tail. ● Sits across perch, long bill/head forwards, body angled, tail projecting.
● Flight supremely elegant: sweeps and flows, with fast rise on quick beats of long, stiff wings, then stall and slow curving glide with wings outstretched.

Sandy plains, open ground, woodland edge.

Roller

PMH 141

Coracias garrulus

Large with stout bill; square head on crow-like body, squared tail. ● Looks quietly down from perch, then drop-pounces on to ground, returning to original perch. ● Flight easy, high, with quick, paddling wing-beats and flashing colours.

Open ground, scrubby hillsides, dunes.

Hoopoe

Upupa epops

Quick *poo-poo-poo*
PMH 141

Quite large. ● Unmistakable, long-bodied; waddles on short legs, slender bill probes quickly. ● May fan crest, bob and flirt tail. ● Explodes into flight; broad wings and butterfly-like wing-beats; dipping/dancing over distance, head up, or swoops into cover.

Agricultural land, parks, woodland edge, pastures.

Wryneck
Jynx torquilla
Too big for warbler, too small for thrush. ● Short spiky bill;
small, neat, round head; rather long, broad tail. ● Elusive,
secretive, well camouflaged. ● Creeps about. ● Flies with
tail prominent; wings flicked, slightly undulating.

Rapid, nasal *kwee-kee-kee-kee*
PMH 141

Forests, forest edge, bushy dunes, parks.

juv

Green woodpecker
Ringing, laughing *keu-keu-keu-keu*
PMH 142; LWS 182

Picus viridis
Large, rather untidy, angry. ● On ground, leaps and hops
jerkily, probes for ants; on trees, hides cleverly behind
branch, peeps round. ● Climbs upright, propped on tail.
● Flight bounding, dropping low from tree, then swooping
away with bursts of wing-beats and closed-wing swoops;
sweeps upwards to new perch.

Deciduous woods, heaths, dunes, pastures.

Black woodpecker

PMH 142

Dryocarpus martius

Very large. ● Striking, tapered bill on large head with angular crest at nape. ● Head held up, often drawn back, on thin neck; long oval body and stiff, rather long, pointed tail. ● Flight powerful, slightly bounding with quick, strong beats.

Mature forest of pine, beech; parkland.

juv

Great spotted woodpecker

Dendrocopos major

Medium-sized. ● Stocky, striking, confident. ● On branches propped up on tail, or hangs beneath; leaps along in jerky hops or dives to next branch. ● Flight swooping in deep switchbacks, shooting up to slap against next perch.

Abrupt *tchik*
PMH 143

Woodland of all kinds.

Lesser spotted woodpecker

Dendrocopos minor

Midget, weak, nervous. ● Sits 'frozen' at times. ● Flits and jumps about on thin upper twigs or in low undergrowth, but typical stiff woodpecker shape. ● Flight flitting in wavering undulations as if undecided where to head.

High, peevish *kee-kee-kee-kee*
PMH 144

Deciduous woods, wooded parks and gardens.

109

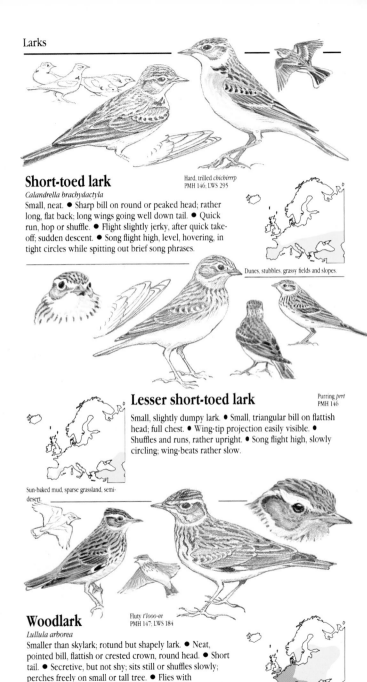

Short-toed lark

Hard, trilled *chichirrrp*
PMH 146; LWS 295

Calandrella brachydactyla

Small, neat. ● Sharp bill on round or peaked head; rather long, flat back; long wings going well down tail. ● Quick run, hop or shuffle. ● Flight slightly jerky, after quick take-off; sudden descent. ● Song flight high, level, hovering, in tight circles while spitting out brief song phrases.

Dunes, stubbles, grassy fields and slopes.

Lesser short-toed lark

Purring *prrt*
PMH 146

Small, slightly dumpy lark. ● Small, triangular bill on flattish head; full chest. ● Wing-tip projection easily visible. ● Shuffles and runs, rather upright. ● Song flight high, slowly circling; wing-beats rather slow.

Sun-baked mud, sparse grassland, semi-desert.

Woodlark

Fluty *t'looo-ee*
PMH 147; LWS 184

Lullula arborea

Smaller than skylark; rotund but shapely lark. ● Neat, pointed bill, flattish or crested crown, round head. ● Short tail. ● Secretive, but not shy; sits still or shuffles slowly; perches freely on small or tall tree. ● Flies with characteristic floppy swoops; wings round and broad, tail very short. ● Song flight slowly circling.

Heaths, forest clearings, sparse woodland.

Chirruping *chrrup*
PMH 147

Skylark
Alauda arvensis

Bigger than sparrow; stout bill, head bluntly crested. ● Tail medium-length. ● Rather bold walk, or crouched in round-shouldered wander. ● In flight, tail looks shorter than broad-based wings, their hind edge straight, fore edge angled back to slightly squared tip. ● Flight strong, slightly undulating; flocks may circle fields and scatter. ● Fluttering before landing. ● Astounding hovering song flight, as if pulled up on string.

Moors, dunes, meadows, ploughed fields.

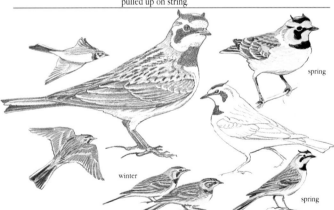

spring

winter

spring

Shore lark
Eremophila alpestris

Shrill *seep*
PMH 148; LWS 185

Quite large, neat, crouched lark, quiet and unobtrusive.
● Mouse-like but always on the move while feeding, then sudden flight; quick and agile for short distance before sudden collapse on to ground. ● Thin wing tips and tail.

Mountain tops, tundra; tide-line marsh, shingle.

High *tswit, tswee-wit*
PMH 149

Swallow
Hirundo rustica
Quite small summer sprite. ● Elongated, with squat head,
long wings and body, spiky tail streamers. ● Sits across wire
or aerial, squatting on ground/roof. ● Flight easy, swooping,
swerving gracefully low over ground, with elegant rowing
of swept-back wings.

Farms, meadows, lakes and rivers, open
ground.

Red-rumped swallow
Hirundo daurica

Rough *chew-ic*
PMH 149

Medium-sized. ● Tiny bill on small, neat head; tapered
body; long tail streamers slightly shorter, thicker than
swallow's. ● Flies with wings rather straight, broad-based
and martin-like, set well forward; tail and under tail coverts
give 'stuck-on' effect against rump. ● Wing-beats shallow,
rather quick and stiff, between long glides.

Warm slopes, open ground around villages.

Sand martin

Dry *tchirrip*
PMH 148

Riparia riparia

Small, slight, flickery; long wings but shortish, forked tail.
● Flight easy and adept, but slightly weak and fluttering,
with jerky back-flick of wings. ● Flocks swarm on wires,
even flat ground; roost in dense reeds.

Earth and sand cliffs; quarries, reservoirs.

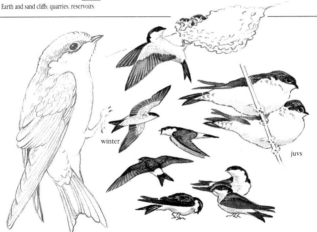

winter

juvs

House martin

Chattering *tchirrip*
PMH 149

Delichon urbica

Quite small, compact; barrel-bodied, with forked tail, rather
broad-based wings. ● Clings under eaves, sunbathes on
roofs, sits on wires. ● Flies high, circling, stiff, with flutter/
flicker of straight wings and frequent flat glides.

Suburbia, villages, open space, reservoirs.

113

Strident *tswee-eep*
PMH 152; HTV 162

Yellow wagtail

Motacilla flava

Smallest wagtail. ● Neat, full-chested but tapered to rear; spindly-legged; tail medium-long, bobbed. ● Neat, quick walk; fluttering runs; short aerial chases after flies. ● Flies in sweeping arcs, rising and falling with bursts of wing-beats; tail fanned on landing. ● Busy parties, often around livestock.

Lake and reservoir edges, old meadows, floods.

juv

Grey wagtail

Sharp *tchik*
PMH 153   winter

Motacilla cinerea

Longest wagtail. ● Slender, tapered, with over-long, fanned tail swung up and down. ● Short, pale legs. ● Quick walk, short leaps from rock to rock. ● Flycatching sallies frequent. ● Flight quickly rising then zooming off in series of long, shallow bounds, tail whipping. ● Not gregarious.

Wooded or open streams; mill races, rocks.

juv

♂ pied   ♂ white

Pied wagtail

Rolling *tsuwee*, hard *tchissik*
PMH 153

Motacilla alba

Chestiest wagtail. ● Neat, bustling bird with long wagged tail. ● Rather long, thin, black legs. ● Runs and walks with high-stepping 'stop-start' over level ground or jumps from stone to stone in streams. ● Aerial sallies after insects.
● Flight direct, with shallow swoops in time with wing-beat bursts.

Gravel pits, lawns, suburbia, parks, streams.

Richard's pipit

Anthus novaeseelandiae

Strong, rasping *schreep*, quieter *shroo*
PMH 150; HTV 153; FBI 114

Large, robust pipit, with skylark-like bulk but long tail.
● Stout, thrush-like bill. ● Legs long and stout, with big feet, very long hind claws. ● Stance often exaggeratedly upright – chest out, head back. ● Confident, long-striding, strutting walk. ● Flight strong, rising quickly and bounding off; dives down, then flutters just above ground before final landing.

Wet grassland.

Tawny pipit

Anthus campestris

tsweep and *chup*
PMH 150; HTV 153; FBI 114

Large, quite stout pipit but more elongated and wagtail-like than Richard's. ● Bill long and pointed; legs long, hind claw long but arched. ● Stance usually rather horizontal but can puff out chest and stand tall. ● Wagtail-like shuffle or quick walk. ● Flight wagtail-like, bounding, lacking weight of Richard's.

Dunes, warm grassy slopes; scrub.

115

Tree pipit
Anthus trivialis

Wheezy *teez*
PMH 151: HTV 156; LWS 188

Smallish, neat, graceful, pipit with deep, clear flanks.
● Quite strong bill. ● Shy-looking, but confident, tall walk.
● Escapes to tree canopy. ● Fluent actions continue into
air where flight strong and rhythmic. ● Not gregarious.

Heathland with bushes; woodland edge, clearings.

typical   western

Meadow pipit
Anthus pratensis

Repeated *peet, peet, peet*
PMH 151: HTV 156

Small, weak-looking, with round shoulders, full breast and
belly. ● Demure-looking; fine bill, spindly legs. ● Shuffling,
mouse-like creep; twitching tail. ● Escapes to grass
tussocks. ● Erratic wing-beats in weak flight, rising in series
of jerky steps. ● Gregarious.

Moors, dunes, pastures, salt marshes, fields.

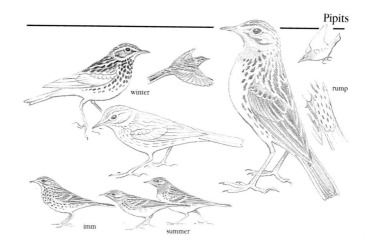

winter

rump

imm

summer

Tundra, moors, coasts; marshes on migration.

Red-throated pipit
Anthus cervinus

High, strained *pseeee*
PMH 152; LWS 297

Smallish, stocky, broad-backed pipit; less chesty but deeper-bellied than meadow. ● Rarely perches; walks easily, lightly, often in coarse grasses. ● Flight quick, strong and confident, often escaping to far distance.

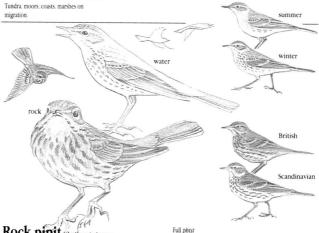

summer

winter

water

rock

British

Scandinavian

Rock pipit *(Anthus petrosus)*

Full *phist*
PMH 152; HTV 159

Quite large, robust, with full tail. ● Bill and dark legs strong. ● Wing-beats full and strong, in sweeping flight.
● Clambers over rocks, searches seaweed; flicks tail.
● Pairs, small groups.

Water pipit *Anthus spinoletta*

pheet
HTV 159

Large, upright, heavy pipit; rather wagtail-like (even wheatear-like) appearance due to plumage patterns, stance.
● Shy; flies up at a distance, going high and far off.
● Usually solitary in winter.

rock pipit is coastal
N. Europe

water pipit range
Water: high pasture, marsh; pools.
Rock: rocky coasts; saltmarsh

117

Great grey shrike

PMH 191; HTV 201

Lanius excubitor

Large, with strong bill, big round head, long tail. ● Angled, or upright on perch, tail waved or stuck out to one side. ● Elusive, or stands out a mile. ● Flight a quick, splashed flurry of wings, undulating over long distances. ● Solitary.

Open, bushy places; scrub, woodland edge.

Lesser grey shrike

PMH 190; HTV 201

Lanius minor

Medium-sized. ● Thick bill on large, round head. ● Upright; thickset body; noticeably long wing points and medium-length tail. ● Rather stiff, immobile compared with great grey; perches prominently; drops to ground or sallies out after prey.

Open bushy places, scrub, woodland edges.

Red-backed shrike

PMH 190; HTV 199

Lanius collurio

Medium-sized, long-tailed. Often inactive, sitting upright, head down, tail hanging or flirted to one side. ● Dashes out to catch insect, or pounces on to ground. ● Flight hurried, low, with whirring beats of blunt wings; tail trailing, often fanned; upward swoop to perch.

Scrub, bushy places, heaths.

juv

Woodchat shrike

PMH 191; HTV 199

Lanius senator

Quite large, stocky, bullheaded, hang-tailed. ● Sits upright, often on prominent perch or hides. ● Knocks down insects, small birds, in sudden flurry. ● Flight low, before sweeping up to a perch.

Bushy slopes; farmland, scrub.

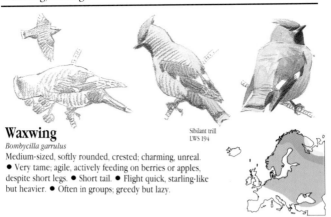

Waxwing

Sibilant trill
LWS 194

Bombycilla garrulus

Medium-sized, softly rounded, crested; charming, unreal.
● Very tame; agile, actively feeding on berries or apples,
despite short legs. ● Short tail. ● Flight quick, starling-like
but heavier. ● Often in groups; greedy but lazy.

Woods, hedges, berried bushes in gardens;
parks.

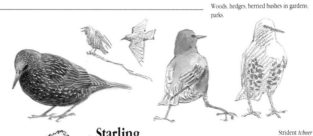

Starling

Strident *tcheer*
LWS 234

Sturnus vulgaris

Medium-sized, sharp-faced, bustling bully. ● Pointed bill
and head on long oval body; triangular wings; short, square
tail; rather long legs. ● Jaunty walk or run. ● Sings with
wings waving loosely. ● Flight strong. ● Fast downward
glide to ground; direct bee-line of high, single bird towards
nest; and swirling, smoke-like evolutions of large flocks all
distinctive.

Suburbia, farmland, woods, fields.

Rose-coloured starling

PMH 196

Sturnus roseus

Starling size but softer outline owing to shorter bill,
rounder head. ● Basic actions starling-like but flight a little
slower; often mixed up in starling flocks.

Fields, open country.

120

juv

Dipper

Cinclus cinclus

Hard *zit*
LWS 194

Medium-sized but compact ball with hunched head, short tail, strong legs and feet. ● Bouncing dip of whole body as if on spring. ● Always by water; walks, jumps, even falls into it from mid-flight; swims or dives under, pops up like cork. ● Flight low, whirring, direct or swerving.

Tumbling streams, wooded or open.

Wren

Troglodytes troglodytes

Harsh churrs
LWS 194

Tiny, irritable, cocky. ● Rotund body with upright tail.
● Creeps and crouches under cover, pops out on to edge to scold observer, then flits away. ● Flight low and whirring, over short distances.

Woods, parks, gardens, moors, islands, cliffs.

121

display

Dunnock
Prunella modularis

Shrill *tseek*
LWS 196

Small, retiring, shuffler. ● Trips or creeps over ground near bushes or through undergrowth. ● Restless; lightning-quick flirts of wing and tail. ● Small groups wave wings in unique semaphore action. ● Flight warbler-like.

Deciduous woods, parks, gardens, moors.

Alpine accentor
Prunella collaris

PMH 155

Lark-sized; unobtrusive, shuffling but confident behaviour.
● Slim bill; stocky, stout; longish tail. ● Flight quick, fluent, dipping, before final dive behind rocks.

High-altitude meadows, rocky slopes, crags.

Robin

Thin *tsee, tic tic-ic*
PMH 156

Erithacus rubecula

Rather small. ● Perky, confident bully. ● Rotund in winter, slims in summer. ● Thin bill, spindly legs, often cocked tail. ● Hops and flits over ground or drops through branches; stands upright, then dips forwards to hop a few feet or pounce forwards. ● Flight flitting, but quick, strong; skips along ground before dives into bush with raised tail if disturbed.

Woods, forest edge, hedges, parks, gardens.

Nightingale

Brilliant song; harsh croak
PMH 157

Luscinia megarhynchos

Quite small, refined, rather rounded, with slim bill; wide-eyed look. ● Strong hops under thick cover, stopping with flicked wings, raised tail. ● Sings from deep cover, often in open on Continent. ● Flight robin-like but faster, full tail.

Dense deciduous thickets, bush heaths, coppice.

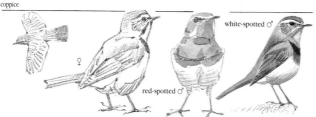

white-spotted ♂

♀

red-spotted ♂

LWS 196

Bluethroat

Luscinia svecica

Robin-like, secretive hopper through low, wet growth.
● Upright stance, forward dips and tilts, flirt of tail.
● Flight quick, direct, sweeping low into cover; looks broad-tailed.

Willows and bushy swamps, reed-beds.

123

spring/autumn

Oak- and beech-wood, rocky slopes with bushes.

Redstart

buveet
LWS 199

Phoenicurus phoenicurus

Quite small, but trails tail. ● Smooth, gentle head profile; full chest tapering to slim, quivering tail. ● Upright; rather quiet; often high in trees. ● Flight a short, quick dash, tail-flash catching the eye; undulating over longer distance.

Black redstart

Stuttering *tititic*
LWS 198

Phoenicurus ochruros

Dumpier, weightier than redstart but similar flattish head, slender rear. ● Dirty-looking, ground-loving. ● Tail flicker frequent. ● Stands up, with sloping back and tail. ● Brisk hop and quick run. ● Flight like redstart but trails tail less.

Crags, boulder slopes, old villages, cities.

Whinchat

wheet-ic
PMH 159; LWS 200

Saxicola rubetra

Rather small, compact, but rather long/heavy-headed.
● Sloping or more horizontal stance; often on weed top above surrounding vegetation. ● May bob and flick wings.
● Flight low, quick, direct and whirring.

Bushy heaths, grassy or heathery plantations.

Stonechat

whee-chak-chak
LWS 200

Saxicola torquata

Rather small but busby-headed. ● Robust, upright, standing on guard on top of stem, or on wire. ● Restless, irritable, inquisitive. ● Hops about, scolds, jerks wings and tail in fit of fury near nest. ● Flight quick, buzzing but agile.

Gorse, heather, bushy places near coast.

125

Wheatear

wheet-chak-chak
LWS 202; BB 80:137, 187

Oenanthe oenanthe

Medium-sized, smart, alert, self-confident. ● Bobs and flirts wings and tail. ● When feeding, short run or hops, then dip, then upward stretch. ● Long wings reach well down tail.
● Flight quick, dashing, low; swoop or flurry before landing shows off winking tail/rump.

Boulders, dry-stone walls near pastures, moors.

Desert wheatear

PMH 161; BB 80:137, 187

Oenanthe deserti

Rather small, pale, rounded and compact. ● Fond of low perches but ground-hugging. Hops. ● Flies off to dip out of sight behind rock.

Stony, sandy and bushy semi-desert.

Black-eared wheatear

PMH 161; BB 80:137, 187   spring/autumn

Oenanthe hispanica

Medium-sized but slim, rather elegant with round head and long, slender tail. ● Perches on tall stems; hops on ground with springy action, dipping tail. ● Flight low, swooping, agile.

Sunny, scrubby or stony slopes, quarries.

Fieldfare

Turdus pilaris

Chattering *tsak tsak tsak*
PMH 165

Large, bold, handsome. ● Long-tailed and rakish on ground/in air. ● Upright stance; often eagerly seeks berries. ● Flocks escape to nearby tree-top. ● Flight loose; floppy bursts of wing-beats between short glides with wings closed. ● Very gregarious, noisy.

Woodland glades, mixed farmland, hedgerows.

drop from tree top

Mistle thrush

Turdus viscivorus

Rattled, dry *tchrrr-chur-chur*
PMH 166

Very big, aggressive, assertive. ● Long-tailed and chesty. ● Upright stance and long, leaping, powerful hops. ● Flight high, easy, with long closed-winged swoops and bursts of wing-beats. ● Sociable in autumn, otherwise rather solitary.

Woodland edge, farmland, parks, large gardens.

Ring ouzel

shek-shek-shek
PMH 163; LWS 204

Turdus torquatus

Medium-sized, elegant, slender, long-tailed thrush; head often raised, tail half-cocked, wings drooped or flicked.
● Flight fast, swooping, with long wing point, sharp-cornered tail. ● Wild, restless at all seasons. ● Whizzes up and down crags.

Upland crags, boulders, bracken slopes, moors.

Blackbird

Startling alarm rattle
PMH 164

Turdus merula

Medium-sized, comfortable, quite tubby. ● Tail often tilted slowly or cocked upright. ● Hops and runs, stops to look.
● Flight low, hurried, thrashing through foliage or dashing across clearing, with initial panicky, noisy explosion, uneven beats.

Woods, farmland, gardens, parks.

Rock thrush

PMH 162

Monticola saxatilis

Small; rather stout, pointed bill on large head. ● Stocky body, short, broad tail; stout legs. ● Stiff, solid actions. ● Flies with quick flurry, but song flight rises in lark-like flutter before graceful, gliding descent in broad sweep; wings pointed, triangular; tail fanned.

Alpine pastures, high crags, sunny slopes

Blue rock thrush

PMH 162

Monticola solitarius

Medium-sized. ● Bill straight, rather long, pointed, often uptilted from sloping forehead. ● Long-bodied but short-legged; medium-length tail. ● Peers out from behind rock; catches insects like giant flycatcher. ● Wings long and pointed, looking full and slightly blunt in flight, elastic; head slightly outstretched, raised.

Crags, boulders, rocky ravines, old buildings.

Redwing

Turdus iliacus

Small, gentle, shy and nervous. ● Rakish face. ● Greedy flocks in hedges or spread across fields. ● Escapes quickly, rising to top of tree or tall hedge. ● Long flights fluttery, lark-like, in flocks. ● Migrants excited, noisy.

Thin *seee*
PMH 166; LWS 206

Birch woods, forest clearings; farmland.

Song thrush

Sharp *sip*
LWS 206

Turdus philomelos

Quite small, typically upright garden bird. ● Rounded, short-tailed, leans forwards in short run or hop forwards, then stops to look and listen. ● Rounded, short-tailed. ● Flies off low into close dense cover. ● Longer flight even, with few glides.

Woods, gardens, parks, mixed farmland.

Cetti's warbler

Forceful, rapid, musical outburst
PMH 167

Cettia cetti

Medium-sized. ● Squat, stout-legged. ● Flicks and cocks broad, rounded tail. ● Skulking, creeping in low growth, tipping forward to dive into cover. ● Flight low, quick; round tail fanned. ● Explosive voice is giveaway.

Dense thickets beside swamps, reed-beds.

High, fast, ticking song
PMH 168

Grasshopper warbler

Locustella naevia

Small. ● Elongated, with rounded tail. ● Skulks in low vegetation; creeps through tangled undergrowth, sometimes cocking tail. ● Runs like mouse in dense cover. ● May sing from open perch. ● Short, flitting flight with 'bucking' tail movements.

Bushy, grassy places, damp moors, wet heath.

Savi's warbler

Low, fast, buzzing song
PMH 169

Locustella luscinioides

Medium-sized. ● Rather heavy build, with long, broad, rounded tail and long under-tail coverts. ● Creeps or sidles upwards through reeds. ● Sings from exposed perch; falls out of sight if disturbed.

Reed-beds and willow thickets.

imm

Aquatic warbler

HTV 176

Acrocephalus paludicola

Rather small, slim. ● Skulks very low, even on ground.
● Short, spiky tail. ● Stands up with legs more visible than
sedge. ● Jerky, low flight, looks slighter than sedge.

Reed-beds and thickets.

ad

Sedge warbler

Chattering, varied song
PMH 170; HTV 176

Acrocephalus schoenobaenus

Rather small but robust. ● Skulks but creeps out of cover to
inspect/scold intruder. ● Agitated, becomes irascible.
● Sidles upwards through reeds and nettles. ● Flight low,
jerky, with tail fanned, depressed; dives into depths of
cover. ● Song often in dancing, rising flight.

Reeds, nettles, willow herb, in swamps,
ditches.

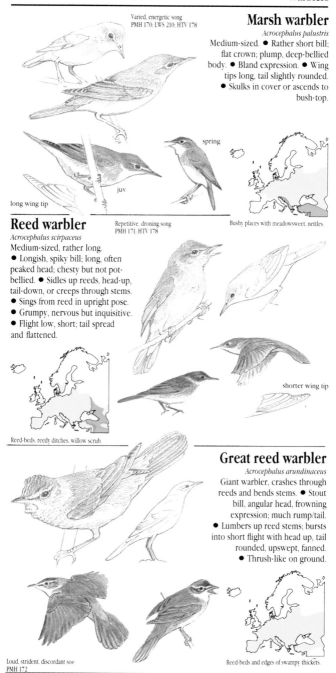

Marsh warbler

Acrocephalus palustris

Medium-sized. ● Rather short bill; flat crown; plump, deep-bellied body. ● Bland expression. ● Wing tips long, tail slightly rounded. ● Skulks in cover or ascends to bush-top.

Varied, energetic song
PMH 170; LWS 210; HTV 178

spring

juv

long wing tip

Bushy places with meadowsweet, nettles.

Reed warbler

Acrocephalus scirpaceus

Medium-sized, rather long.
● Longish, spiky bill; long, often peaked head; chesty but not pot-bellied. ● Sidles up reeds, head-up, tail-down, or creeps through stems.
● Sings from reed in upright pose.
● Grumpy, nervous but inquisitive.
● Flight low, short; tail spread and flattened.

Repetitive, droning song
PMH 171; HTV 178

shorter wing tip

Reed-beds, reedy ditches, willow scrub.

Great reed warbler

Acrocephalus arundinaceus

Giant warbler, crashes through reeds and bends stems. ● Stout bill, angular head, frowning expression; much rump/tail.
● Lumbers up reed stems; bursts into short flight with head up, tail rounded, upswept, fanned.
● Thrush-like on ground.

Loud, strident, discordant song
PMH 172

Reed-beds and edges of swampy thickets.

133

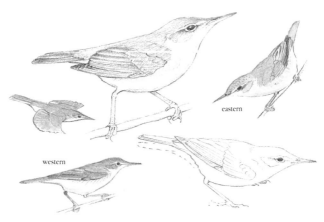

eastern

western

Olivaceous warbler

Sparrowy *tec tec*
PMH 172; FBI 41

Medium-sized, pot-bellied but quite delicate. ● Long, spiky
bill, flat head. ● Short wings; narrow, square tail frequently
dipped. ● Restless.

Bushy places, tamarisk, willows near reeds.

brown

Booted warbler

FBI 41; HTV 181

Small. ● Spiky bill rather weak, held upwards; head domed.
● Wings short, tail square; pot-bellied. ● Subdued, even
sluggish, often very low down.

Bushes, undergrowth near
coasts.

typical ad

imm

Icterine warbler

Short *teck*
LWS 210; HTV 181

Hippolais icterina

Rather large; bill long, dagger-like, broad-based, and long forehead gives beaky look. ● Abrupt vent, square tail.
● Clumsy hops/leaps, make vegetation sway; tugs at berries.
● Strong flight shows long wings.

Woods, bushy places.

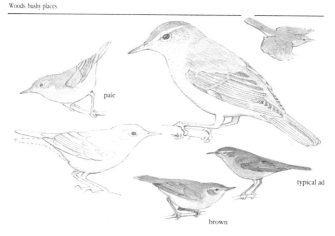

pale

typical ad

brown

Melodious warbler

Sharp *tic*, sparrowy chatter
LWS 210; HTV 181

Hippolais polyglotta

Not obviously big or heavy, but plump, with abrupt vent.
● Tail square. ● Bill quite long, broad-based, on usually rounded head. ● Bold movements through foliage but often skulks. ● Wings rather short; flight more fluttery than icterine.

Woodland edge, scrub, bushy places.

Barred warbler *Sylvia nisoria*

Big, heavy, robust; plenty of tail.
● Bill thick; steep forehead, staring eye in adult. ● Tail long, square-cornered, flicked and swayed.
● Skulks, often immobile, then hops to top of bush. ● Flies low but straight across gaps in short, jerky, powerful bursts.

imm

ad

Garden warbler

Sylvia borin

Medium-sized. ● Plump, rounded, gentle-looking. ● Plain, obscure features.
● Stubby bill, dark eye, bland, rounded face. ● Shy but shows well when singing in trees and tall shrubs. ● Flight quick, jerky, heavier than blackcap.

Blackcap *Sylvia atricapilla*

Medium-sized. ● Thin-billed, flat-headed, slim, restless. ● Flits through foliage but in autumn feeds on berries, less mobile except for occasional heavy leap. ● Sings from high perch, body trembling, throat extended.
● Flight jerky and quick; tail fairly long, narrow, square.

Barred warbler

imm

ad

PMH 176

Garden warbler

Hard or softer *tak*
PMH 177; LWS 214

Blackcap

♂

♀

Hard, abrupt *tak*
PMH 177; LWS 214

Woodland edge, dense thickets, bushy places.

Deciduous woods, scrubby clearings, old hedges.

Deciduous woods, parks, bushy clearings.

Lesser whitethroat

Loud, hard, rattled song
LWS 212

Sylvia curruca

Rather small, neat and tidy, with shorter, slimmer tail than whitethroat. ● Noticeably compact. ● Skulks in dense thickets; male often high in trees when singing. ● Enjoys juicy berries in autumn. ● Flight lighter, more direct than whitethroat, with tail held tight.

Tall, dense hedges and thickets.

Whitethroat

Scolding *charr*
LWS 212

Sylvia communis

Medium-sized; more chest than belly, so slim, with long, loose tail. ● Pale eye, peaked crown give annoyed look. ● Restless, skulking then leaping up into open, flitting across bush-top, diving back head first with tail cocked or flirted. ● Usually low in thorny tangle, or on wire; song flight brief, upward-bouncing.

Heaths, scrub, gorse, bramble thickets, hedges.

spring ♂

imm

Subalpine warbler

PMH 174

Sylvia cantillans

Small; *Phylloscopus*-like shape. ● Short bill, peaky head, puffy throat. ● Longish, slim tail flicked and cocked. ● Skulking, but looks back from cover. ● Short, jerky, whirring flight; dancing song flight.

Bushy slopes, dense thickets.

♂

imm

Dartford warbler

Soft, churring *charrr*
PMH 174

Sylvia undata

Small, slim but can look round-bodied. ● Peaky crown, puffy throat give large head; chest scarcely deeper. ● Tail long, slim, half total length, often raised, flicked or waved sideways. ● Secretive, but hops out to bush-top before diving in again. ● Short, low, jerky, skipping flight on very short wings.

Heather and gorse on sunny heaths; scrub.

Siberian

juv   short

Chiffchaff

Phylloscopus collybita

Soft *huee*
HTV 189

Small, rounded; wings and tail rather short. ● Seemingly short bill on rounded head; legs look spindly. ● Constant wing flicking; wags tail. ● Often very low, but sings high in trees.

Deciduous woods, willow thickets.

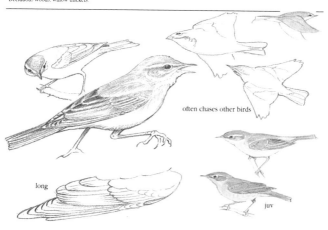

often chases other birds

long

juv

Willow warbler

Phylloscopus trochilus

Soft *boo-eeet*
HTV 189

Small, slim, light-weight; active. ● Flattish head; rather long wings and tail. ● Wings flicked; flits restlessly or slides quietly through foliage. ● Occasional fly-catching sally. ● Flight low, weak-looking but quick and agile; often chases small birds.

Woodland, clearings, bushy areas.

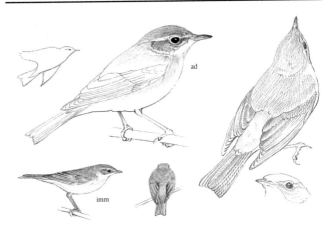

Bonelli's warbler

tchu-weet or *chiup*
PMH 179

Phylloscopus bonelli
Small, sleek; head rather large, tail narrow. ● Wings rather pointed. ● Slips easily through foliage of bushes, pine-trees. ● Shyer than willow, feeding in cover; flight like willow.

Oak or pine forest.

Wood warbler

High, ticking trill
PMH 179

Phylloscopus sibilatrix
Medium-sized and rather long. ● Pale, prominent bill on large head; long, pointed wings often drooped beside square tail. ● Usually high in trees, moving in short jumps or fluttering beneath canopy ● Flight light and airy.

Oak-, beech-, larch-woods with sparse undergrowth.

Pallas's warbler

wee-eest
PMH 178

Phylloscopus proregulus

Tiny, dumpy, large-headed and short-tailed. ● Neckless, rounded shape and stripes recall firecrest. ● Flights short, quick, buzzy, with frequent hovers; restless, often making vertical drops and flutters inside foliage.

Trees.

Yellow-browed warbler

Shrill *tchuweee*
PMH 178

Phylloscopus inornatus

Tiny, slender but large-headed. ● Shape like small willow. ● Slips quietly and unobtrusively through foliage, often with goldcrests. ● Frequent short, quick, rather bouncing/dashing flights. ● Hovers to feed from outer leaves.

Trees. scrub.

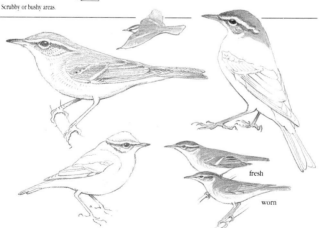

Greenish warbler

Thin *che-wee*
HTV 189

Phylloscopus trochiloides

Small, rather rounded with prominent eye, large, rakish head; light-weight. ● Often skulking, unobtrusive. ● Call unlike Arctic; flight like chiffchaff.

Scrubby or bushy areas.

fresh

worn

Arctic warbler

Hard *tzik*
PMH 177; HTV 189

Phylloscopus borealis

Small but robust with strong bill, flattish/rakish head, rather long wings, strong, pale legs. ● Quick, active movements, abrupt changes in height give mercurial mien. ● Flight stronger than willow.

Scrub and woodland edge.

Goldcrest

Regulus regulus

Thin, high *see-see*
PMH 181

Tiny, rounded, neckless and short-tailed. ● Minute bill, prominent eye; rather dirty. ● Flicks wings. ● Restless flitting and short, busy flights; equally at home in high or low foliage. ● Oblivious to human presence.

Mixed woods, conifers in parks, large gardens.

Firecrest

Regulus ignicapillus

Sharp *seet*
PMH 181

Tiny, startlingly beautiful, clean; head and tail longer-looking than goldcrest's. ● Often keeps very low; less restless than goldcrest. ● Hovers.

autumn passage

Mixed woods, conifers, bushy places.

143

Spotted flycatcher

Muscicapa striata

Sharp *tzee*
LWS 218

Medium-sized, featureless but ever-alert. ● Long wings, longish, thin tail, short legs. ● Sits upright, then darts out, twists and turns to snatch fly, returns to same perch. ● Likes interfaces of light/shade.

Open woods, clearings, parks, churchyards.

imm

♂

Red-breasted flycatcher

LWS 218

Ficedula parva

Small, delightful, confiding and endearing. ● Short bill, round head; slim wing tips droop beside raised, thin tail. ● Dashes out from perch to snap at fly or drop momentarily to ground. ● Flies 'tighter circle' than others.

Coastal woods and gardens in autumn.

♀

spring ♂

♀

Pied flycatcher

Ficedula hypoleuca

Sharp *wbit*
LWS 218

Medium-sized with large, rounded head; compact body slopes, tapering down to slim tail. ● Slips through trees, flits out to catch insects mid-air, lands on new perch. ● Drops to ground frequently.

Open oak-woods with sparse undergrowth.

Bearded tit

Panurus biarmicus

Small, but full-bodied, long-tailed. ● Unique reed-bed bird.
● Conical, waxy bill; rounded head with narrow, domed
crown. ● Whirrs over reeds like tiny pheasant. ● Often in
noisy groups, restless and mobile.

Ringing or kissing *ping*
PMH 183

Reed-beds; rarely other swampy places in winter.

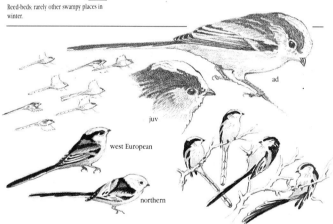

Long-tailed tit

Aegithalos caudatus

Unique, tiny, ball-and-stick shape owing to round body,
long pin-tail. ● Light and delicate but rather stiff form; flits
and jumps. ● Small flocks cross clearings line astern or in
dribs and drabs with bouncing flight.

Colourless *see-see-see*
PMH 183

Woodland edge, bramble thickets, hedges.

145

Marsh tit

Bright, sharp *pitchew*
HTV 196

Parus palustris

Small, sleek, well turned out; restless, jerky, active. ● Large head, slender body. ● Bends forwards to peck at food, often held in feet. ● Secretive, in trees, also flits down to lower undergrowth. ● Joins tit flocks.

Deciduous woodland, beech spinneys, parks.

British

Scandinavian

Willow tit

Buzzing *airr-airr-airr*
HTV 196

Parus montanus

Small but looks robust and slightly untidy, with big head and bull neck. ● Active, bold, leaping out and in along thickets and hedges, swinging about low stems. ● Noisy. ● Often in pairs, rarely joins other species.

Swampy woods, willow thickets, old hedges.

Continental

Coal tit

Ringing *tseu*
LWS 222

Parus ater

Tiny, light-weight ball, with short stick-tail; always neckless, head round and large or sleek and slim. ● Creeps and hops about high twigs, but also explores ground, holes in walls, rough bark. ● Zooms to peanut bag, stops dead from full-speed, zooms off again with nut.

All kinds of woods, conifers in parks.

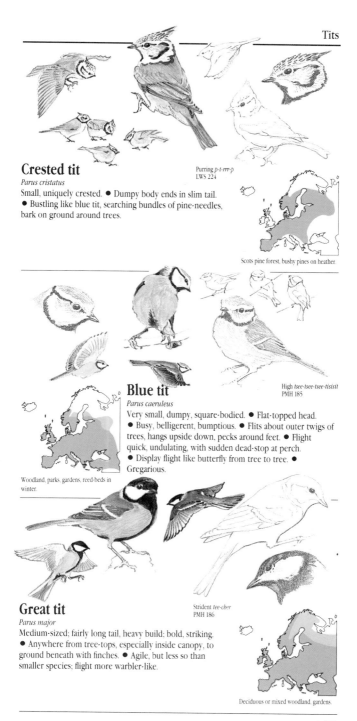

Crested tit
Parus cristatus

Purring *p-t-rrr-p*
LWS 224

Small, uniquely crested. ● Dumpy body ends in slim tail.
● Bustling like blue tit, searching bundles of pine-needles,
bark on ground around trees.

Scots pine forest, bushy pines on heather.

Blue tit
Parus caeruleus

High *tsee-tsee-tsee-tisisit*
PMH 185

Very small, dumpy, square-bodied. ● Flat-topped head.
● Busy, belligerent, bumptious. ● Flits about outer twigs of
trees, hangs upside down, pecks around feet. ● Flight
quick, undulating, with sudden dead-stop at perch.
● Display flight like butterfly from tree to tree. ●
Gregarious.

Woodland, parks, gardens, reed-beds in
winter.

Great tit
Parus major

Strident *tee-cher*
PMH 186

Medium-sized; fairly long tail, heavy build; bold, striking.
● Anywhere from tree-tops, especially inside canopy, to
ground beneath with finches. ● Agile, but less so than
smaller species; flight more warbler-like.

Deciduous or mixed woodland, gardens.

Nuthatch

Rapid whistling *twee-twee-twee-twee*
LWS 226

Sitta europaea

Medium-sized, unbalanced form owing to long bill, deep
flanks, short tail. ● Jaunty, strange. ● Jumps jerkily along
bark, up, along, down head-first, using feet, not tail. ● Sways
head, bobs and flicks wings. ● Noisy, inquisitive. ● Flight
flitting, dipping; lots of head/wing but no tail in silhouette.

Mature deciduous woods, old parkland
trees.

Treecreeper

Thin *seeee*
HTV 197

Certhia familiaris

Small, slim, tree-bound. ● Ghostly, sudden appearance/
disappearance. ● Creeps up bark of tree, spiralling round
branch or trunk, then flits down to next and starts again.
● Mouse-like, jerky shuffle, propped up on tail; can hang
beneath with feet alone. ● Flight weak, flitting, looking
long-tailed.

All kinds of woods, parks, tall hedges.

Yellowhammer

Emberiza citrinella

Sharp *twitik*
LWS 246

Large bunting, chesty but slim, with long rear body/tail.
● Sharp bill, small eye, low, flat forehead give strained
expression. ● Feeds on ground; perches prominently,
flicking cleft tail. ● Flight quick, rather direct after long,
sloping ascent.

Gorsy heaths, bushy commons, farmland.

Cirl bunting

Emberiza cirlus

Insignificant *sip*
LWS 247

Rather small, slim, secretive bunting. ● Drooping, pointed
bill, peaky crown. ● Feeds on ground, shuffling quietly,
crouched, unobtrusive. ● Perches on wires, tall trees; sings
from bush-top. ● Flight weak, undulating/irregular, often
horizontal into cover.

Hedgerows, farmland, sparsely wooded
slopes.

Corn bunting

Miliaria calandra

Dry, spluttering jingle
LWS 248

Bigger than sparrow, thickset. ● Thick bill on large, round
head. ● Perches openly with head hunched down, body
rounded/ruffled, untidy hanging tail. ● Flutters away,
losing height to settle on ground some way off, often after half-
circle. ● May dangle legs in display. ● Sparrow-like on
ground. ● Long distance flight high, strong, undulating.

Cereal fields, extensive pastures, bushy
slopes.

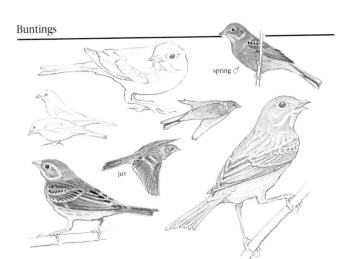

spring ♂

juv

1st autumn

♂ spring

♀

spring/autumn

Ortolan bunting

tsee-ip
PMH 208

Emberiza hortulana

Rather small, neat, noticeably slim. ● Large eye with pale ring, flat head, blob-bill give questioning expression. ● Shy; often on ground, hopping, flicking tail. ● Sits immobile on bush when singing. ● Flight quick and direct.

Grassy pastures, high-altitude meadows.

Yellow-breasted bunting

Thin *tik*
PMH 209

Emberiza aureola

Oddly small, compared with common buntings. ● Peaky crown; compact body and rather short tail. ● Flies like small chaffinch, lacking wing flirts/loose tail.

● Inconspicuous, staying in/close to cover.

Scrub, marshes.

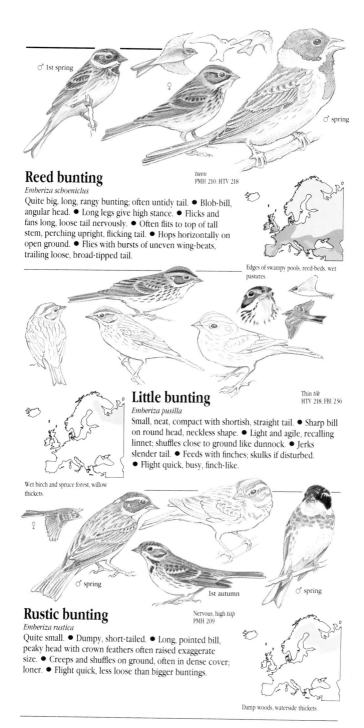

Reed bunting

Emberiza schoeniclus

tseeu
PMH 210; HTV 218

Quite big, long, rangy bunting; often untidy tail. ● Blob-bill, angular head. ● Long legs give high stance. ● Flicks and fans long, loose tail nervously. ● Often flits to top of tall stem, perching upright, flicking tail. ● Hops horizontally on open ground. ● Flies with bursts of uneven wing-beats, trailing loose, broad-tipped tail.

Edges of swampy pools, reed-beds, wet pastures.

Little bunting

Emberiza pusilla

Thin *tik*
HTV 218; FBI 236

Small, neat, compact with shortish, straight tail. ● Sharp bill on round head, neckless shape. ● Light and agile, recalling linnet; shuffles close to ground like dunnock. ● Jerks slender tail. ● Feeds with finches; skulks if disturbed. ● Flight quick, busy, finch-like.

Wet birch and spruce forest, willow thickets.

Rustic bunting

Emberiza rustica

Nervous, high *tsip*
PMH 209

Quite small. ● Dumpy, short-tailed. ● Long, pointed bill, peaky head with crown feathers often raised exaggerate size. ● Creeps and shuffles on ground, often in dense cover; loner. ● Flight quick, less loose than bigger buntings.

Damp woods, waterside thickets.

151

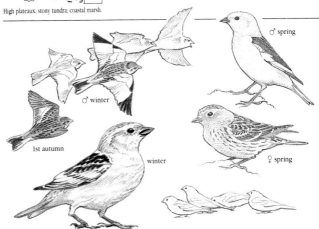

autumn

Lapland bunting

Hard rattle and full *teuu*
PMH 206; HTV 218

Calcarius lapponicus

Big, appearing skylark-sized. ● Long, heavy body, short legs, long wings and short, neat, cleft tail. ● Creeps like mouse, runs on ground like snow. ● Flushes close, with sudden burst; flies fast and direct with flickering, long wings; often gains height. ● Joins snow buntings, finches, larks.

High plateaux, stony tundra; coastal marsh.

Snow bunting

Rippling trill, liquid *tew*
PMH 206; LWS 244

Plectrophenax nivalis

Big, chunky, as long as skylark. ● Short legs, long wings give low-slung carriage; runs and shuffles on ground.
● Frequent short flights, leap-frogging to front of feeding flock. ● Flight strong, swooping on long wings; flocks fly up suddenly to dance in fast, bounding undulations, then drop to ground suddenly as if 'switched off'.

High crags, boulder fields; tundra; coasts.

autumn

Blackpoll warbler

PMH 205; LWS 322

Dendroica striata

Size, build, stance recall willow warbler but chestier, with long wing points and tail. ● Long, active sprite; rather plain face but etched wings and winking tail spots. ● Flight flitting; feeds at all heights.

Trees, scrub.

autumn

Red-eyed vireo

LWS 322

Vireo olivaceus

Size and build recall garden warbler but bill longer, face marked, legs stocky. ● Inactive, 'grubbing' from leaves, looks depressed. ● Stance horizontal. ● Flight quite strong, flitting heavily; feeds in canopy.

Woodland.

153

Continental

Chaffinch

Fringilla coelebs

Lively *pink*; dull *chup*
PMH 199

Medium-sized but lengthy. ● Stocky head and chest but longish body, wings and tail. ● Bright and cheerful. ● Wings flash in flight. ● Hops along twigs, then drops to ground to creep inconspicuously. ● Flocks get up few at a time, fly loosely grouped to cover, or up into trees above. ● Flight strong, but flitting, undulating.

Woodland of all kinds, parks, gardens, fields.

juv

♂ spring

♂ winter

♀

Brambling

Fringilla montrifingilla

Nasal *tswink*, hard *tchup*
PMH 199

Medium-sized, very like chaffinch, but tail shorter, more forked; pointed, triangular bill, slightly peaked head and full chest a bit more obvious. ● Flocks similarly loose, unco-ordinated. ● Flight fast, bounding, often high.

Birch-wood, beeches, fields and hedgerows.

Siskin

Carduelis spinus

Twanging, metallic *tsy-ee*
PMH 201

Small, elegant, slender, sharp-faced, acrobatic tree-top bird.
● Sharp wing points, deeply forked tail. ● Flocks co-
ordinated, dashing out of tree if disturbed, zooming off in
fast, rhythmic undulations, swerving back again when coast
clear, settling as one bird.

Coniferous and mixed forest; alders,
birches.

Serin

Serinus serinus

Jingling twitter
PMH 199

Tiny, stumpy, fluttering finch. ● Stubby bill, beady eye, flat
head; short tail. ● Hops about twigs, grovels in
undergrowth or sways about on stems. ● Flight bouncy,
dancing, but quite fast.

Village gardens, parks, farmland copses,
fields.

Goldfinch

Carduelis carduelis

Liquid, twittering twitter
PMH 200

Rather small, light and airy, bouncing, delicate. ● Sharp, lengthy bill; bold face. ● Swings round thistle-tops, teasels. ● Flight very lively, dancing in deep, erratic undulations, in tight groups. ● Large flocks swoop round and round over weedy fields.

Parkland trees, avenues, rough ground, thistles.

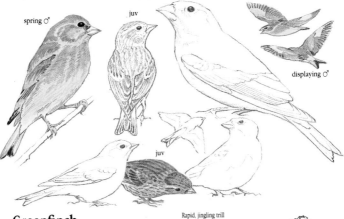

Greenfinch

Rapid, jingling trill
PMH 200

Carduelis chloris

Medium-sized but stocky, with heavy body, short legs. ● Deep bill and mask give frown. ● Sits about, swings on nut bags, chomps berries; not very agile on ground or among slim stems. ● Flocks fly up together, quick, bounding. ● Song-flight bat- or butterfly-like.

Bushy hedges, clearings, parks, gardens.

156

British

juv

Continental

♂ winter

Greenland

Continental

British

Redpoll
Carduelis flammea

Hard, chattering *chuchuchuch*
PMH 202; HTV 210

Tiny, dumpy, blunt-faced, fork-tailed finch. ● Likes birch/alder/willow but often on ground or in tall weeds, clinging to stems. ● Flight tight, even, with bounding undulations but 'knows where it's going' in well co-ordinated flocks.

Plantations, scrubby woods, bushy places.

winter

1st winter

ad winter

1st winter

Arctic redpoll

PMH 202

Carduelis hornemanni

Slightly heavier, longer-looking, flatter- or more dolphin-backed than redpoll, with tiny bill, feathery 'shorts'.
● Ghostly; restless, with bounding flight.

Willow and birch thickets, woodland edge.

Linnet

Carduelis cannabina

Light, spluttering trill
PMH 201

Small, slim, neat; squarish head. ● Highly strung.
● Triangular bill. ● Perches low; feeds on ground. ● Flight
wavering, bouncy, flocks in tight, dancing packs which often
pause to twitter musically from bush-tops.

Bushy heaths, hedges, rough ground, fields.

Twite

Carduelis flavirostris

Twanging *twaaee*
PMH 201

Subtle, streaky; small bill and head, long wings and tail.
● Short legs. Ground-loving; tight-knit, bounding flocks
wheel up then pour down to disappear again in vegetation.

Rough moors, coastal or hill pasture, salt
marsh.

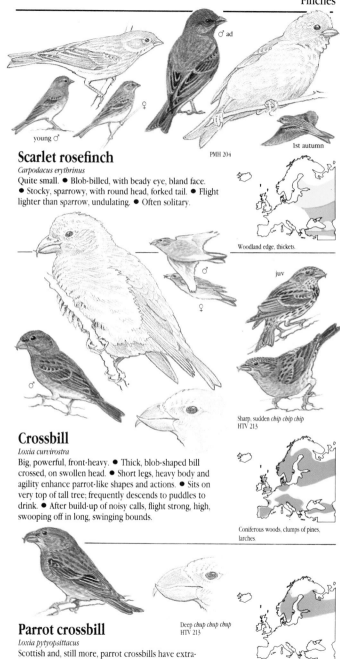

Scarlet rosefinch

Carpodacus erythrinus

Quite small. ● Blob-billed, with beady eye, bland face.
● Stocky, sparrowy, with round head, forked tail. ● Flight
lighter than sparrow, undulating. ● Often solitary.

PMH 204

young ♂   ♀   ♂ ad   1st autumn

Woodland edge, thickets.

Crossbill

Loxia curvirostra

Big, powerful, front-heavy. ● Thick, blob-shaped bill
crossed, on swollen head. ● Short legs, heavy body and
agility enhance parrot-like shapes and actions. ● Sits on
very top of tall tree; frequently descends to puddles to
drink. ● After build-up of noisy calls, flight strong, high,
swooping off in long, swinging bounds.

♂   ♀   juv

Sharp, sudden *chip chip chip*
HTV 213

Coniferous woods, clumps of pines,
larches.

Parrot crossbill

Loxia pytyopsittacus

Scottish and, still more, parrot crossbills have extra-
muscular head and neck, bulging cheeks, massive bills.

Deep *chup chup chup*
HTV 213

Conifers.

159

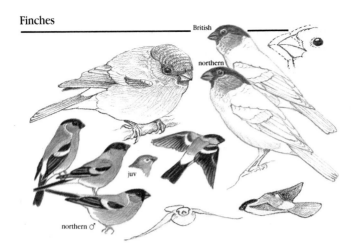

British

northern

juv

northern ♂

Dense hedges, orchards, thickets, gardens.

Bullfinch

Piping *peu peu*
PMH 204

Pyrrhula pyrrhula
Rather big, dumpy quiet, self-effacing. ● Short, blunt bill;
round, low-profile head. ● Full wings; narrow, oblong tail.
● Sits still but explores all cover to collect buds, seeds.
● Flight low, quickly concealed in cover.

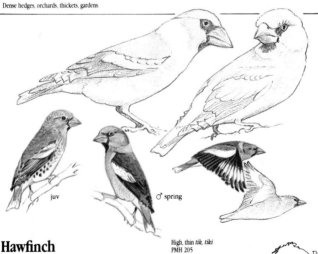

juv

♂ spring

High, thin *tik, tiki*
PMH 205

Hawfinch

Coccothraustes coccothraustes
Big, front-heavy, dynamic but shy, elusive. ● Massive bill,
deep belly, broad tail and short legs suggest parrot. ● Sits
high on tree-top in full view, dropping quietly to forest
floor to feed. ● Massive bill, deep belly, broad tail and short
legs. ● Flight high, fast on long, pointed wings, sweeping
over, then into tall woods.

Bushy woodlands, beeches, parkland.

House sparrow
Passer domesticus

Familiar chatter
HTV 216

Medium-sized, compact, perky and cheery, cheeky, cocky, familiar but quick to take alarm. ● Hops about in jerky fashion, or sits making a noise, in thicket. ● Not very agile but has a go at any food source. ● Flight fast and direct.

Towns, villages, parks, suburbia, farmsteads.

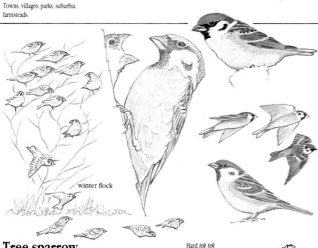

winter flock

Tree sparrow
Passer montanus

Hard *tek tek*
HTV 216

Rather small, dumpy, smart and handsome, with stout bill, neat, round head. ● Tail often half-cocked. ● Flight faster than house, often towering escapes. ● Secretive, but joins finches and buntings in fields.

Old trees in farmland and parks, coastal fields.

Golden oriole

Fluty *wheela-wheeo*
PMH 189

Oriolus oriolus

Large, loose, splendid yet elusive, more heard than seen.
● Slips through broadleaf canopy allowing glimpse of
rather long, thrush-like, peculiar bird. ● Leaping hop.
● Short flights through canopy, or drops beneath to clear
space, sweeps rapidly on, and shoots back upwards into
cover.

Dense woodland, poplar plantations,
willows.

Magpie

Staccato, harsh chatter
PMH 193

Pica pica

Large, lengthy, country character, with swaying, long, active
tail. ● Canny, missing no trick. ● Hops among branches, or
leaps over ground in series of long, springy bounds.
● Flight direct, with fairly quick wing-beats, looks short of
lift. ● Often in small groups.

Farmland, suburbia, woodland edge.

Jay

Tearing, shrieking *shairk*
PMH 192

Garrulus glandarius

Large, with 'expanding' wings and tail in flight. ● Gleaming eye, jerky crest, sharp, confident movements give a jaunty, bold air. ● On ground has long, jumping hops and bounds. ● Flight quick and low into cover, or slower, more laboured over woods at a height. ● Secretive except where safe in parks, then tamer.

Woodland of all kinds, parks, large gardens.

Nutcracker

PMH 193

Nucifraga caryocatactes

Large, peculiar, strange. ● Stout, pointed bill; long, heavy body and broad wings combine with short tail to give odd proportions perched or flying. ● Jaunty, springy movements. ● Flight rhythmic, undulating.

Mountain conifer forests, forest clearings.

Chough

Pyrrhocorax pyrrhocorax

Squeaky, ringing *kee-yaa*
PMH 193; LWS 230

Medium-sized, ebullient crow. ● Long, down-curved bill from slender, pointed face. ● Body tapered but closed wings add bulk, reach well down tail. ● Jaunty walk, hops; explores turf with probing, teasing bill. ● In air, tapered head, but shortish, slightly wedge-tipped or square tail and deeply-fingered, squared wings. ● Flight bouncy, dynamic, bounding; soars with ease, dives down cliff face and swings back in up-draught, or zooms with closed wings.

Coastal and inland cliffs, maritime heath.

Jackdaw

Corvus monedula

Squeaky *tchak*
PMH 194

Smallish, neat, characterful crow. ● Short, stout bill, peaky head. ● Ambling, cocky gait; looks neat and well turned out. ● Flight quick, direct; wings set well forward, slightly tapered and rounded, with easy, even rowing action. ● Also glides and dives excitedly around cliffs and buildings.

Woodland, fields, parks, buildings, cliffs.

display

Rook

Pleasant *kaaa*
LWS 232

Corvus frugilegus

Rather large, homely, elderly-looking, with sharp-pointed bare face, loose flanks that spray in waddling, yet long-striding walk. ● Bill steadily probes. ● Delights in tree-tops, leans into strong winds, jerking tail and flicking wings. ● Competent soaring, direct flight heavier, slow, with steady beats of rather pointed wings; rounded tail.

Woodland edge, fields, upland moors.

hooded

carrion

Carrion/hooded crow

Harsh, often triple *caa*
LWS 232

Corvus corone

Big, handsome, impressive, menacing air. ● Stout bill, flat forehead on bold face. ● Tight body plumage. ● Direct flight heavy, slightly laboured; head fairly short, wings square or fingered, tail square.

Moors, fields, woods, waste ground.

mid-air roll

Raven

Loud, resonant croaking; *tonk tonk*
LWS 232

Corvus corax

Huge, very strong, angular, domineering. ● Big, arched bill, bristly throat, huge head. ● Throat feathers can be raised. ● Strong legs, powerful gait. ● Direct flight level, steady, long wings angled back, tail diamond-shaped; but soars, dives, even rolls on back. ● Primaries closed or fingered, warped to create loud noise.

Upland moors, crags, coastal cliffs.

Index

A

B

C

R

S